ECOLOGY

CRISIS
AND
NEW VISION

edited by
Richard E. Sherrell

John Knox Press
Richmond, Virginia

International Standard Book Number: 0-8042-0819-0
Library of Congress Catalog Number: 72-156300
© John Knox Press 1971
Printed in the United States of America

FOREWORD

This volume of essays grew out of a symposium occasioned by an attempt to look upon the growing ecological and environmental crisis as an opportunity for new vision. Beginning, perhaps, with the implicit challenge for response from the religious community laid down in Professor Lynn White's charge that the Judeo-Christian tradition is primarily to blame for the present sorry state of our environment, the concept of the symposium matured through several discussions among concerned university faculty people. The basic assumption underlying the symposium was that the ecological crisis was too important to leave to the ecologists. What was needed were some imaginative handles with which to grasp the, by now, almost overwhelming data of the crisis situation. A group of sensitive people were gathered to explore the elements of a new vision with which to see our situation, and to point to some of the resources in the religious traditions of both East and West to shape such a vision. The agencies sponsoring the symposium were the Church Society for College Work (Cambridge, Massachusetts) and the Department of Higher Education, National Council of Churches (New York City).

To assert that the ecological crisis is too important to leave to the ecologists alone is a deliberately provocative statement. The crisis of our human environment is perceived by the man in the street to have something to do with the interdependence of living things with their habitats. Scientifically, it is the ecologists who know most about this interdependence, both for humans and for nonhuman organisms. Most of us have begun to learn a little of what the ecologists know, and in proud possession of a little knowledge identify our environmental crisis as one of ecology. Let it be said right here that we do our ecologist colleagues an injustice if in making this identification we seem to imply that it is somehow their fault, since it has to do with their field of special competence. Often enough, scientists

are insensitive to the social implications of their knowledge, but in
the present instance it has been the scientists who have been sound-
ing the warning Klaxon for a decade and more. But let it also be said
that, while ecologists can tell us much about food chains and the
proper management of plant and animal populations, as ecologists
they cannot tell us *why*—that is, for what human, social, and spiritual
purposes—we as men should survive the havoc we have wreaked
upon our environment. The solution to this question requires a different vision, not unrelated to what ecologists, technologists, economists, perhaps even politicians and industrialists can tell us, but a new
vision, a different vision from the ones which have guided our cultural growth to the present.

New vision is not easy to come by. To even raise such a question
immediately conjures up images of poets and religious mystics. Certainly, we need these people as desperately as other imaginative
sorts, but most of us "men in the street" don't read the poets very
much, to our own great loss. We do, however, pay some attention
to scientists and even to a few theologians, and among these imagination is by no means lacking. Several names come quickly to mind
—René Dubos and Loren Eiseley among scientists, and Harvey Cox
and John Cobb among theologians. These men, together with a host
of others, are beginning to shape the elements of a new vision which
gives promise of answering the dilemma of why and how man is to
survive. The present volume gives voice to some of that larger host
of sensitive persons who are taking seriously the challenge of
imaginatively wrestling with the environmental crisis.

It is not by chance that when we speak of the environmental (or
ecological) crisis, we are really talking about the human environment. The Western religious traditions have been roundly criticized
(both rightly and wrongly) for having perpetrated a view of the
"natural" (i.e., nonhuman) world which makes it subservient to the
wants of man. And yet it is precisely the human situation in the midst
of the natural world that concerns most of us—we perceive ourselves
as a threatened species. To be sure, the threat seems largely to be
one of our own making; hence, we feel guilty about it, but it is
primarily *our* environment that concerns us. Thus, the so-called
environmental movement is not really grounded in ecology—a matter of changing environments and of new species replacing old ones

—but we are largely involved in an anti-ecology concern for the survival of one species, man (as we mostly know him, *Homo sapiens*). From an ecological point of view, there is no reason why *Homo sapiens* should not evolve into something else as his environment changes. Or he might just die out as other species before him have done when they could not adapt to new conditions. Most of us won't settle for these alternatives, however committed we may be to the cold comfort of scientific knowledge about most other matters in our lives. We want to survive, and both our human biology and our religious feelings suggest we are valued by a source of power greater than ourselves. Thus, we are concerned for the human environment.

At the same time, the human environment is more than air, water, and forests; mountain lions and microorganisms; city streets, superhighways, and country lanes. We live in a social environment in which our covert assertion of man's value above other things is worked out in human relationships, ethically and unethically. Our cultural development to the present in the West has proceeded upon the assumption that at least some men are more important than the things they manipulate, including other men. In consequence, we have built a consumer society which has only recently begun to worry about the trashy by-products of its affluence. Unfortunately, so long as the environmental crisis is seen in terms of production and pollution, and the ability among the affluent to pay for both, there are large segments of the society left untouched in their economic and social plight by this analysis. It is the minority poor among us who see the environmental crisis neither as their own problem, nor as one which should take precedence over fundamental questions of social justice. From the perspective of the poor, the affluent decision-makers of our society seem to be posing the alternative of pollution control *or* aid for urban poverty, and that is a bad choice. On the one hand, there is every reason for the poor to believe that the choice will go against them and for what the suburban middle class sees as desirable—more trees, cleaner air, purer water—for the suburbs, that is. On the other hand, to pose this kind of alternative says nothing about what continues to be *the* number one priority among the affluent—national defense and military budgets. On both counts, the minority poor perceive the environmental crisis as largely irrelevant to their own situation *unless* the crisis is broadened to take into account the social dimensions of the human environment. If we continue to treat people the way we treat things, the social environment will not change.

Together with questions of social ethics, the environmental crisis presents us with problems both within ourselves and in the extensions of ourselves we call technology. Traditionally, religion has addressed itself to the great source of human anxiety, death. As traditional religion has lost its grip upon our imaginations, we have replaced it with both good science and bad. Good science, and its implementation through technology, has vastly improved the conditions of daily life. Bad science—among other things it has deluded us into believing—has strengthened our desire to avoid facing up to the fact of death. A consumer society seems peculiarly, if also perversely, designed to complement this avoidance. We not only collect immense amounts of military hardware, we just plain collect things against the gnawing suspicion that despite our wealth and power and technology we will die. If we are to come to terms adequately with the environmental crisis in which too many things and people threaten us all, then we must come to some kind of terms with an unacknowledged fear of death which profoundly undergirds our personal and corporate responses to our world.

Men have always participated in their environments, and have manipulated them from the first tool until now. Modern technology is very much with us, and we must use it with all the creative imagination we can muster. The alternative facing us has to be more complex than that between the SST and the cave, as some romantics would seem to pose it. To be sure, there is a sense in which the power of technology is mystical to many, and, certainly, awe inspiring to all of us. But we can ill afford either to worship it or hope it will go away. It is not enough to blame the environmental crisis on technology, though technology has been used in part to create it. Nor is it enough to believe that just more technology of the kind we have been using will save us or our environment. We have got to use different technologies for better ends. It is a human problem we face, since all our technology is an extension of our minds and bodies. Technology is not neutral, any more than any human creation is neutral; our values inform our making of it, and our values determine our use of it. Technology in turn affects those values which do function in our culture. Even on the question of the human use of technology, then, we return to religious questions—who is man, what is his worth and purpose, what is valuable in life—and to the need for new vision with which to grasp our environmental situation.

These several themes—the realities of the ecological and environmental situation, and the philosophical and theological issues they raise; the questions of social ethics and economic justice in the larger human environment; the problem of death; the humane uses of technology; the resources of religious imagination in dealing with problems of human values—cut across all the essays of this present volume. In sorting out personal approaches to the larger environmental issue, the several participants focused upon one or another of the themes in order to deepen its contribution to new vision. Out of the discussions a fairly logical order to the essays emerged in three subsections: Environment as Problem; The Wider Human Environment; Resources of the Religious Imagination. It is in the midst of the essays that new vision begins to emerge. The cumulative statement of this volume is neither precise nor final—it is an effort to open up new ways of viewing our environmental situation. If the essays lead their writers to further work, and lead their readers to further reflection and action, they will have made their contribution to new vision.

A special debt of gratitude is owed to Myron B. Bloy, Jr., and Joseph L. Walsh of the Church Society for College Work, neither of whose names appear on the table of contents, but without whom the original symposium would not have happened. And especial thanks are hereby expressed to Mrs. Marion I. Sinclair for her careful and arduous work in preparation of the manuscript.

RICHARD E. SHERRELL

CONTENTS

THE AUTHORS

THADIS W. BOX is Dean of the College of Natural Resources, Utah State University, Logan, Utah. Born and educated in Texas, Dr. Box is a prolific writer, especially in the field of range management. He has lectured in Australia and India, and was honored in 1967 by the Danforth Foundation in receiving the E. Harris Harbison Award for Distinguished Teaching.

NORMAN J. FARAMELLI is Associate Director of the Boston Industrial Mission, Cambridge, Massachusetts. Born and educated in Pennsylvania, Dr. Faramelli worked as a chemical engineer before becoming ordained a priest in the Episcopal Church. He has been a visiting lecturer at Andover-Newton Theological School.

EVERETT E. GENDLER is a staff member of Packard Manse, an ecumenical center in Stoughton, Massachusetts. Born in Iowa and educated in Chicago and New York City, he was ordained a Rabbi at Jewish Theological Seminary. Having served congregations in Mexico and Brazil, he has worked with Centro Intercultural de Documentacion (CIDOC) in Cuernavaca, Mexico, and briefly served Jewish congregations in Cuba. He has published articles in several journals and serves on the faculty of Havurat Shalom Community Seminary, Somerville, Massachusetts.

SCOTT I. PARADISE is Executive Director of the Boston Industrial Mission, Cambridge, Massachusetts. Born in Massachusetts and educated at Yale University and the Episcopal Theological School, Mr. Paradise is a priest of the Episcopal Church. He has served on the staffs of the Sheffield Industrial Mission, England, and the Detroit Industrial Mission, Michigan. He has contributed to journals and book editions, and in 1968 published *Detroit Industrial Mission* (New York: Harper and Row).

MICHAEL ROSSMAN is alive and well and living in Berkeley, California. Born and educated in California, Mr. Rossman left academia in the mid-sixties to work at campus organizing and publishing. He is particularly concerned with education.

JOHN H. SNOW is Episcopal Chaplain at Princeton University. Educated at Harvard, Columbia, and the Episcopal Theological School, he is an ordained priest of the Episcopal Church. He has served parishes in Massachusetts and for two years was Executive Director of Gould Farm, Monterrey, Massachusetts. He is both an author and lecturer.

DAVID F. K. STEINDL-RAST is a monk at the Benedictine monastery of Mount Saviour, near Elmira, New York. Born and educated in Vienna, Austria, Brother David holds the Ph.D., has been a Post-Doctoral Fellow at Cornell University, and has been a student of Zen Buddhism under Hakuun Yasutani Roshi. He has lectured and published widely, and is especially concerned with the role of monks as bridge builders between East and West.

RICHARD A. UNDERWOOD is Associate Professor of Philosophy of Religion, The Hartford Seminary Foundation, Hartford, Connecticut. Born in Kansas and educated in Indiana and New Jersey, Dr. Underwood has taught at Upsala College, Drew University, and Stephens College. He has lectured widely and contributed to journals and edited books.

PART ONE

Environment as Problem

o

1

ECOLOGY AND NEW VISION: A BIOLOGIST'S VIEW OF PHILOSOPHICAL AND THEOLOGICAL ISSUES

Thadis W. Box

For almost a century the science of ecology has been studied, practiced, and taught by a small but growing group of biological scientists interested in the relationship between organisms and their environment. Recently, the science has been thrust into the newspaper headlines and man's relationship to his environment has been discussed widely in the mass communications media. The science of ecology and ecologists themselves have been thrust into leadership roles in the current concern for man's environment, and the relatively new field of human ecology has emerged. Although the same principles of ecology apply to flower beetle populations in a laboratory environment and to human populations in an urban ghetto, the field of human ecology is complicated by psychological, social, philosophical, and theological factors not readily apparent in lower animals. Therefore, today's ecologist needs not only to be a well-trained biologist, but to have new vision and insight into social, psychological, and theological issues. The purpose of this essay will be to outline briefly man's ecological situation in the world today and raise some social and theological issues which must be answered before the biologist can adequately apply his ecological knowledge to human populations.

Man's current concern for his environment is not a new phenomenon. Historically, he has raised issues about a particular part of his environment from time to time. Here in America we are actually experiencing our third major ecological movement. The earliest occurred near the end of our frontier era when most of the land available for settlement had been occupied. It was exemplified by a concern for saving portions of the frontier and the establishment of reserved areas that could be utilized by future generations. Champions of this movement, such as Theodore Roosevelt and Gifford Pinchot, were successful in calling to the attention of the American public the need for the establishment of national parks, national forests, and other areas that would protect given land surfaces from the ravages of man.

The second major ecological movement in this country occurred during the mid-thirties when a series of events including drought and expansion into land not ecologically suitable for intensive agriculture caused huge dust bowl areas throughout our country. Concern for the endangered landscape resulted in the establishment of the U.S. Soil Conservation Service and a very successful program of land reclamation. In both cases, the ecological concern was for localized areas of a rural landscape rather than the total environment, and the solutions were thought to lie in more conservation programs rather than any total ecological awareness. However, there have been prophets who pointed out that conservation was much more than the saving of a particular piece of landscape, and that ecological principles should be applied to conservation. In 1941, the late Aldo Leopold wrote:

Mechanized man, having rebuilt the landscape, is now rebuilt
the waters. The sober citizen who would never submit his watch or his
motor to amateur tamperings freely submits his lakes to drainings,
fillings, dredgings, pollutions, stabilizations, mosquito control, algae
control, swimmer's itch control, and the planting of any fish able to
swim. So also with the rivers. We constrict them with levees and dams,
and then flush them with dredgings, channelizations, and the floods
and silts of bad farming. . . . We perceive organic behavior only in those
organisms which we have built. We know that engines and governments are organisms; that tampering with any part of them may affect
the whole. We do not yet know that this is true of soils and water. Thus
men too wise to tolerate hasty tampering with our political constitution
accept without a qualm the most radical amendment to our biotic
constitution.[1]

Thus Leopold clearly spelled out that man is a part of his total
environment and operates under the laws of ecology.

In his book *Road to Survival,* William Vogt in 1949 brought
ecological thinking to focus on man's total environment and indicated at the time that population increase and environmental
deterioration would lead to man's extinction. He wrote that unless
"man readjusts his way of living in the fullest sense to the imperative
posed by the limited resource of his environment—we may as well
give up all hope of continuing civilized life." These warnings of over
two decades ago have suddenly captured the interest of the general
public and man's ecology has become a major issue.

The current ecology movement differs from the previous ones
in several ways. First, the previous movements were mainly associated with rural land and rural areas. In the current ecological
crisis, the major concern is voiced by non-rural people who are
directly affected by smog, pollution, and deterioration in the ghetto,
problems only emphasized by the success of the space program and
the efficiency of modern communications media. Millions of people
were able to sit in front of their television screens and see the earth
as a small ball floating in space. Academic statements by scientists
indicating that the earth is a closed system with finite resources
suddenly had real meaning to the man on the street. Improvement
of the environment became a major political issue. For the first time
it has become apparent that ecology is not simply a biological technique for studying rodent populations, but a science that has a direct

impact on the very survival of man. It is likewise apparent that man's survival depends on some very difficult decisions about changes that may not be readily acceptable in today's social setting. For instance, many of the changes necessary for solution of the present ecological crisis will affect the major industries of this country and the jobs and livelihoods of many people. Although it may not be so simple as to suggest that the average factory worker must choose between clean air or a pay check, there are elements of truth in this statement. Other changes must be of a very personal nature, affecting the life-styles of people themselves. Not only will man's working and eating habits change appreciably, but even his behavior in the bedroom must be altered if he is to survive. These issues call for a new vision of man himself involving his psychological, social, and religious behavior. Man's current ecological situation can be summarized briefly as too many people, not enough resources, and a population with attitudes bent on exploitation. To cope with this, man must have new vision —a vision geared toward effective population control and a change in mores and attitudes.

THE ECOLOGICAL SITUATION

Man is a part of nature and does not operate separate and apart from the natural laws affecting other organisms. Many of today's ecological problems are the result of ignoring this simple fact. Man is, at best, considered by many people as some sort of separate super-being that sits apart from "nature" and enjoys or exploits it without being part of it; at the worst, he is seen as a being favored by a divine power and subject to being bailed out of any mess he creates by divine intervention. Seldom is man seen as an integral part of nature who must bear the consequences of his ecological action.

If the ecological approach to man is accepted—that he is an animal and a part of nature—then the question of man's significance arises. Is this one animal special? Why is he special? Does he need a personal God? Is he part of some grand plan centered around his species?

Man as a part of nature is on his own. He is part of a closed system where there are too many people living in a habitat with too few resources. He is part of a population of thinking animals whose life-styles and attitudes are directed toward exploitation rather than balance of environmental factors.

TOO MANY PEOPLE

Ever since T. R. Malthus presented his treatise on human population growth, scientists and academicians have argued over his predictions, the slope of his curves, and the reasons why he was right or wrong. Since the recent publication of Paul Ehrlich's book, *The Population Bomb,* world demographic studies have become a major item of public interest and are widely quoted in newspapers, magazines, and other mass communications media. Although demographers may argue about the size of the human population and its exact rate of growth, almost all informed persons know that the world population now exceeds three and a half billion and that it is doubling every thirty-five years. They are further concerned that this population growth is not evenly distributed around the world; but that the major growth takes place in the developing countries, those with less chance of feeding their people.

Although the public is generally aware of the rapid growth, many are not aware of the basic ecological principles of population dynamics governing the growth. Gause, an early ecologist, observed the growth of natural populations of flower beetles in the laboratory. Since that time his work has been projected to most other kinds of living animals. All natural populations in a limited environment tend to follow an S-shaped curve. The increase in population is slow at first as the individuals become established and adjusted to the new environment. Following this adjustment period, numbers increase at a geometric rate until some factor in the environment becomes limiting. At this time a balance between birth and death occurs and the carrying capacity of the environment is established. If the carrying capacity of environment is exceeded due to artificial propagation, most of the population will eventually starve. There is an upper capacity limit on all environments and infinite population growth is impossible.

In order for any population to regulate its numbers in relation to the carrying capacity, it must: (1) reduce the birth rate, (2) increase the death rate until these two values are in balance. Although scientists argue over the ultimate carrying capacity of the earth, and others point out that population projections have often been wrong, no one can deny that the resources of the earth are finite and that the numbers of people that they can support are limited.[2] Even though the level at which the human population must be stabilized can be argued, it is obvious that human population control is the major element in solving the current ecological crisis and that this control will include both birth control and death control. When population is viewed in this manner, *several philosophical and theological issues are raised for which the ecologist does not have the answer.*

Why Should Man Survive?

The first and most obvious issue is: why should the human animal survive? The principle of succession, or the orderly process of community change, is well-established in ecology. New organisms establish themselves and new communities displace old ones as environments change. *The current environmental concern, then, is not an ecology movement,* but an anti-ecology movement concerned with the survival of one species, *Homo sapiens.* In this respect, the survival of man is much like managing a population of bobwhite quail in a forest environment. The population can only be maintained by working against natural succession. The world's total environment is constantly changing. As the environment changes, an animal must evolve to fit the new conditions or it becomes extinct. Biological history is filled with the stories of dinosaurs, saber-toothed tigers, and the like. Endangered species today, such as the whooping crane and the condor, may simply be expressions of species whose environment changes more rapidly than the animal can adapt. Is man simply another species which cannot adapt in the current world?

There is something more valuable about human life than life of other plants and animals. What is this higher value and how is it manifested? The fact that the human animal considers himself favored over other animals does not preclude the use of ecology in the management of man. In fact, ecological principles may be applied to human populations in the same way wildlife biologists apply ecology to the management of game species or a range manager applies ecology to the management of a grassland population. Ecological thinking as well as sociological, economic, and political criteria are valid in establishing the goals and objectives under which a human population is managed. What, then, are the philosophical and theological implications of managing human lives and human populations?

Wildlife managers have long observed the difference between the biological potential (breeding ability) of an animal population and the actual number of animals produced.[3] They indicate that the observed difference is caused by "environmental resistance." They break the environmental resistance down into limiting factors such as food, water, air, etc., and decimating factors such as diseases and catastrophes. If the decimating factors are removed, the population may grow to the point where the limiting factors ultimately control the population. In game management, the objective is to substitute sport hunting for the natural factors of predation, disease, etc. In the human· population, if diseases and predation (murders and war) are removed, the human population will ultimately face starvation through overcrowding. Although we may argue over the exact level of the carrying capacity of the earth, it is evident that the human population must be controlled. A number of theological and philosophical issues are raised here.

Limiting New People

Most of the discussion in theological circles in the past has involved birth control or the prevention of conception. Although this issue is still important and has not been fully resolved, other more delicate moral and ethical questions are raised in population control. For instance, what is the difference between contraception and prevention of birth after conception? If birth prevention, or abortion, is to be practiced, at what age can the fetus be removed without taking a human life? If a fetus can be removed through abortion, why can't children be removed before they contribute appreciably to the welfare of the population? At what age can infanticide be tolerated? Is the time for culling unwanted children three days after conception, three months, six months, two years, ten years? What is meant by human life and at what age does an individual become a person? These questions must be answered in a way acceptable to the majority of the population if the accretion of new individuals into the human population is to be adequately controlled.

Most birth control discussions center themselves around contraception and the prevention of conception. A more realistic approach must necessarily include the changes in attitudes toward sex and the role of the woman in our society. If the population is truly to be controlled, a woman must be liberated from motherhood as a career. Along this line William R. Burch states:

> The present policies regarding sex roles and family life insure that just about everyone will be propelled into reproductive unions, and that half of the population will enter into such unions as a career—a life's work. To gain control on population growth will require reducing marriage and parenthood to marginal rather than central sexual roles. It will also require the removal of restrictions upon abortion, upon sexual unions for pleasure rather than reproduction, and upon homosexual unions between consenting adults, while encouraging the development of viable careers other than motherhood for women.[4]

What are the theological positions on sex for pleasure? Three of the recent top ten in non-fiction books in this country are filled with examples of explicit sex behavior. Some present masturbation, homosexual unions, and casual encounters for pleasure as normal rather than deviant sexual behavior. These practices are clearly feasible and desirable for controlling population, but are not socially or morally acceptable to much of our culture today.

The place of the woman in American society has traditionally been in the home. The redefinition of the role of the woman in our society may be needed if the human population is to be adequately controlled. The old adage of keeping women barefoot and pregnant exemplifies the attitudes of many males toward the role of the female in our society. Motherhood is generally accepted as the only major productive role in which women can take competitive advantage over men. If more careers are made available for women, the population problems may be solved more easily.

Death Control or Removing People

Some advances have been made toward birth control in recent years, but little has been done in the field of death control. Modern medical technology has allowed people to remain in the human population longer than in the past. R. S. Miller states that, "the reason for this time lag between a decline in death rate and a corresponding decline in birth rate in the demographic transition of a population is that death rates are relatively easy to control, and their control is socially acceptable and desirable in modern society, while birth rates are more difficult to influence."[5] Modern medical science has made it possible to save the lives of infants and extend the life of the aged. These successes in medical science are adding to our population problem. Several theological issues are raised around increasing the death rate. Can we cull nonproductive people from the population? Who determines "productivity"? Under what conditions can euthanasia be practiced? These questions are directly related to removing people from the population who are using space and resources, but who are not contributing to the welfare of the population. In ecology, the total welfare of the population is generally considered over the welfare of an individual within the population. The health of an individual member is assumed to be better if the population is in balance with the carrying capacity of the habitat. This "good of the population" rationale is often used for allowing doe hunts in controlling a deer population or extending hunting seasons in years with high quail populations. The health of the individuals in the lowered population is improved, but some individuals are sacrificed. Can the ecological concern for the welfare of the human population be reconciled with the theological concern over the worth of an individual?

Aside from issues involving the actual removal of human beings from populations, death control also involves moral issues of keeping people alive who have contracted a terminal illness. Is it a moral act to prevent a person from dying gracefully? Can society allow affluent people with terminal illnesses to fill hospital beds when space is needed by less affluent members of the labor force?

These issues must be raised in any serious consideration of the application of ecological principles to human populations. Not only are they of ecological importance, but they raise questions of distributive justice and social concern. Those of us in ecology can furnish the scientific knowledge necessary for the manipulation of human populations, but most of us do not want to face the moral, social, and theological issues involved. Neither do we have the training nor background to answer adequately many of the questions raised. In my opinion, the ecologist has the biological principles to help *Homo sapiens* survive, but he needs help in the way that he applies these tools.

NOT ENOUGH RESOURCES

The major reason for restricting human population growth is to keep the population within resources available for them. The last two decades have seen a series of alternating opinions expressed by well-qualified experts on the earth's capacity for food production. For instance, Jonathan Garst's *No Need for Hunger* expressed optimism followed by the Paddock brothers' depressing treatment, *Famine 1975!* Currently, Lester Brown's treatment of the green revolution in *Seeds of Change* expresses a cautious optimism provided certain environmental safeguards are practiced. Before the publication of this book, Dr. Brown was quoted in a population bulletin as saying:

> If the question asked is, "can we produce enough food to sustain, at adequate dietative levels, the projected population increase between now and the end of the century?," then the answer is yes. But, if we ask, "what are the social and ecological consequences in the rapid advances of farm technology which enable us to sustain past and future increases in population?," we get a different answer. Unfortunately, although we can produce more than enough food, we are only beginning to realize that the social costs are painfully high and that the ecological consequences are only beginning to appear. If we succeed in producing more than enough food, but destroy our environment in the process, what will we gain?[6]

Land

It is becoming more apparent that maintaining a human population is more than producing food to sustain it. Only by relating man to the total resource pattern can the ecological picture be understood. G. W. Thomas approached the problem by calculating the amount of land, water, energy, air, and open space needed to sustain a man. His analysis is worthy of examination.[7]

The President's Science Advisory Panel on World Food Supply (1967) estimated that there are about 7.6 billion acres of land in the world that are suitable for cultivation under intensive agriculture and another nine billion with a potential for grazing. These figures are based almost entirely on physical resources of the world, and do not consider the social, political, and economic restraints on production. Taking their figures, only about two acres per person have the potential for intensive agriculture today. Only about half of this, or one acre per person, is actually in agriculture. These figures produced by the President's Science Advisory Council include high mountains occupying about 20 percent of the land's surface; huge deserts, another 20 percent; tropical rain forests and rugged terrain, an additional 30 percent.

It is estimated that with the present technology of developed countries, about one acre per person is desirable to produce enough food for an adequate standard of living. Today only about 11 percent of the earth's land surface is cultivated, or about one acre per person —the recommended base for today's level of technology. These cultivated acres are not equally distributed. For instance, the Far East has only 0.8 acre per person; Communist Asia, 0.4 acre per person; Latin America, about 1.3 acres per person; Africa, about 2.3 acres; and the United States, about 2.4 acres. Traditionally, man has increased his food supply by expanding the area under intensive agriculture. At the present time, there is approximately an adequate balance between the number of acres under cultivation and the number of people on the earth. If the human population is allowed to continue to grow, new acres must be put into cultivation or new technology developed. Both choices could be ecologically costly. Land left for expanding agriculture is that with low potential or with serious management problems. Any attempt to bring new land under cultivation will require additional inputs of fossil fuels, other energy sources, commercial fertilizers, etc., which will result in a further altering of man's environment. Also, in many areas, cultivation effects permanent change in some ecosystems (e.g., tropical and desert areas).

By far the largest amount of land in the world is classified as uncultivated. From this uncultivated land man derives many of his animal proteins, almost all of his forest products, a large percentage of his oxygen supply, a major amount of the water used for irrigation on cultivated lands, and an undetermined benefit from the recreation and aesthetic values associated with wild lands. These multiple use benefits have not been taken into consideration when calculating the amount of land needed to support one person. With our current technology, it appears that man will require approximately one acre of cultivated land to sustain him. In addition, he will make use of the remainder of the land for the various multiple uses discussed above. Any increase in the amount of intensive agriculture will reduce the amount for grazing, water yield, and the intangible aesthetic values.

Water

Water is essential for the maintenance of life and many believe that it will be the first limiting resource in world food production. It has been pointed out that as the standard of living rises so does water consumption. For instance, only about two liters of water a day are needed to maintain human life. However, as early as 1900, home consumption in the United States was about 10 gallons of water per day. Now the annual consumption is near 180 gallons per day. The amount of water increases with the affluence of the user. Automatic washing machines, dishwashers, and garbage disposers all add increased water use. In 1968, residents of Beverly Hills, California, with a per capita income of slightly less than $5,000 per year averaged 315 gallons of water per person per day. This compares with 89 gallons per person per day in nearby Compton, California, where the per capita income is only $1700 per year.[8]

Water in a closed system is periodically recycled through the hydrologic cycle. Although it is never completely lost from the system, water is poorly distributed on the face of the earth and much of it is tied up in unusable forms such as sea water, ice, or brackish underground supplies. While total amounts of water available on the earth cannot be changed appreciably, both distribution and quality can be changed and directly affect the amount of water available for human use.

A recent study of water redistribution systems and the ecological effects of these systems concluded that ecological considerations were far more important to water projects than economic or engineering considerations.[9] Many water transport schemes have been suggested to import water from the water surplus areas and distribute them in the water deficient areas, to alter precipitation, or to desalinate and recycle sea water. Although the engineering capabilities exist for many of these today, little is known about the ecological consequences of the projects. At the present time, it is impossible to evaluate totally the benefits and weigh them against detrimental effects.

Air

Much of the current ecological concern revolves around pollution in the atmosphere. It is embarrassing that we have so little accurate information on the effects of air quality upon man's ecology. We know that certain contaminates are increasing, but little as to their effect. It has been estimated that the mean CO_2 content of the atmosphere has risen from 290 parts per million in 1900 to some 330 parts per million in 1960.[10] The total effect of this rise in carbon dioxide is argued among scientists. Some claim that it produces a greenhouse effect and warms the earth's surface. On the other hand, others contend that the increasing concentration of particles will reflect light and lower temperatures in the earth's surface. R. H. Whittaker stated, "It is indicative of man's inability either to predict adequately or to control his effects on environment that we do not yet know whether the net effect of pollution of the atmosphere will warm or cool the earth's surface or how serious the climatic effects will be."[11]

Some ecologists point to the fact that most of the oxygen supply comes from tiny plants in the ocean and that with increased pollution of the salt water, man could be in an oxygen-short environment in the future. Other studies show that there has been little change in the oxygen content of the atmosphere since measurements were first made. Although there is disagreement on the effects of pollution in the earth's total environment, those people living downwind from a steel plant certainly can attest to the fact that local areas have now become unfit for human habitation!

Energy

Energy, unlike water, is not a major limiting factor in the total earth's ecosystem. If the total energy of the sun could be captured, only one square meter of surface area would be necessary to capture the energy needs equivalent of the food necessary for a man. Unfortunately, only a very small amount of the sun's energy is captured and even less of it goes into final products for man's use. For instance, less than 1/40,000 of the sun's energy falling on an area grazed by a cow in its lifetime is stored in the meat of a cow.[12]

The United States is now the largest user of fossil fuel that the world has ever known. Recent popular articles have pointed to the fact that each American has twenty to fifty times the ecological effect on his environment as someone from a developing country. These reports are based primarily on the use of fossil fuel. When total impact on the basic land resource is considered, the figure is somewhat lower.

Current news releases indicate that the fossil fuel supply in the world is not now meeting the demand. Geologic fuels are now used for almost all of our energy needs. With the exception of a few nuclear reactors, hydroelectric plants, and a small number of solar devices, the majority of man's agriculture, industry, and home comfort devices are powered with oil, gas, coal, or other geologic fuels. In many cases the amount of these fuels expended is greater than the production from the use of the fuel. For instance, it has been calculated that the fossil energy needed for food production alone (excluding the supply, processing, and distribution functions) is more than the energy level of the food that finally reaches the consumer.[13] These figures indicate that if the caloric costs of all activities in American life are added, the fossil fuel uses are in excess of 21,000 calories per person per day, over seven times the level of the caloric value of the average diet.

It appears that we are converting fossil fuels to usable food and services at a very costly rate. Not only is energy dissipated at each transfer, but products released from the burning of fossil fuels act as contaminates to the air. In addition to the atmospheric contaminates released in the burning of fossil fuels, a large amount of heat is lost, causing thermal pollution to rivers, lakes, and the atmosphere.

Open Space

No adequate estimate exists on the amount of open space necessary for a human being. Psychological studies show that crowding of some species leads to abnormal and deviant behavior. Some people have postulated that many of the problems of our cities are caused primarily by the crowding of people. On the other hand, we do not know how much and what kind of space is most desirable for a high quality life. If the human population is to continue to grow at the present rate, these values must be determined.

Theological and Philosophical Issues Raised

It is obvious the resources of the earth are finite and that they must be utilized efficiently if growing numbers of human beings are to be supported. Certain issues are raised that are not strictly ecological, but are philosophical and theological. For instance, who owns resources? Can individual ownership of natural resources be tolerated?; and, if so, under what conditions?

Some suggest that the Judeo-Christian ethic, in particular the statement in Genesis involving dominion over the land, has caused many of our ecological problems. What is meant by dominion over the land? Does this give an individual or society the right to exploit the land for short-time goals?

What are the ethics of using natural resources to maintain high levels of human populations in this generation knowing that there are not enough resources to do so? In many regions of the world, people are now exploiting resources through the mining of minerals or underground water, knowing full well that the mining operation will leave society without the resource and without the option for alternative uses of the resource as the human population grows. Is this action morally acceptable?

As I pointed out earlier, the use of geologic fuels is causing increased pollution of other resources such as air and water. Is it morally justifiable to prevent the use of resources, e.g., geologic fuels, to protect another resource—air?

Many construction projects—roads, dams, subdivisions, etc.— are designed by engineers with little or no consideration for aesthetics or ecology. If aesthetic values are to be protected, projects normally cost more. Is it morally justifiable to take limited public funds from one area, such as welfare, to insure that the beauty of the landscape is protected on a road construction project? How does distributive justice relate to long-term resource supply?

ATTITUDES OF PEOPLE

The whole philosophy of the Western world is geared around growth and development concepts. No program or institution is considered good unless it is growing. Natural resources cannot sit unattended, but must be "developed." Normally, development means exploitation. It is only recently that a few people have begun to realize that the earth is a closed system in which growth cannot continue infinitely. The emphasis is now shifting toward higher quality rather than quantity. This leaves a number of questions unanswered. For instance, what is meant by quality of life? The Australian aborigine in his native state was an example of a man in almost perfect balance with his environment. He led a meager existence in his hunter-gatherer economy and practiced primitive methods of population control to insure that his population did not exceed the carrying capacity of his harsh environment. Yet few people in the civilized world would consider that the aborigine had a high quality existence. Our current foreign aid projects are geared toward changing the life-styles of many people and developing the countries more toward a Western industrialized society. Can we guarantee the quality of our life-style?

Closely associated with the quality of life is the question, what does it mean to be a person? What, if anything, makes the human animal unique and different from another animal, and what must we do to maintain the conditions under which a man can truly be a person?

If the current ecological crisis really calls for a change in life-style, as many of us contend it does, can we safely manipulate attitudes and life-styles without harming the individual as a person? Can we tolerate the brainwashing required to make forthcoming generations accept life-styles necessary for proper land use? It may be necessary to concentrate large numbers of people on small areas, leaving the more productive land available for agricultural purposes. Can we condition people to live happily in ghettos and cage-like situations while leaving the majority of the landscape open and available for production of their food, oxygen, and water?

Can we expect people to accept ecological evidence as criteria for establishing guidelines for life-styles? We have not been successful in the past. Fire is a natural ecological factor and has been used to manipulate man's ecology and his landscape for years. However, because of the prejudice against fire, the banning of this helpful tool has been a standard policy of many of the agencies dealing with land use. For instance, Ashley L. Schiff shows how the U.S. Forest Service became so committed to preventing fires in the forest that it suppressed all evidence as to the value of burning for timberland improvement.[14] The campaign against fire by Smokey the Bear and his forestry colleagues has spread to other agencies and conservation groups to the point that it is almost heretical to suggest that fire is an important factor in maintaining many of our natural environments. The prejudice against fire, coupled with the fact that smoke is a visible contaminate, has caused many restrictions to be placed on burning that will undoubtedly have undesirable ecological repercussions in years to come.

Can the mass media be used to educate or brainwash the public into accepting new values in life-style? If so, whose life-styles?

CONCLUSIONS AND SUMMARY

There can be little doubt that we are living in a time when the concern for man and his environment is at an all-time high. We have finally admitted that the resources of the earth are finite and that we must live within these resources. The use of these finite resources is complicated by a growing human population and an increasing technology. In discussing the relationships between population growth and technology, G. M. Woodwell made the following points:

1. The biotic resources of the earth are no longer large in proportion to the demands man is making on them.
2. Demands on resources, biotic and abiotic, increase with the development of technology. Technology increases the fraction of the earth's surface commanded by an individual. This means that an individual takes up more space on earth if he has technology.

3. Technology increases competition or interference between people, increasing the need for manners or laws regulating behavior.
4. Technology, too, is increasing on an exponential curve. We could measure its doubling time on the basis of the use of fossil fuel, variously estimated as doubling every fifteen to twenty years. Consumption of fossil fuels is only loosely coupled to the increase in population and can be considered as a crude measure of the extension of technology.

Clearly, the environmental crisis is due not simply to an increase in the numbers of people or simply an increase in technology, but to the product of these two exponential curves; population with a doubling time of decades and technology with a doubling time approaching one decade. The doubling time of the environmental crisis is thus measured not in decades, but in years.[15]

Woodwell points out vividly that time is running out, and that action must be taken if man is to survive the current ecological crisis. In his analysis, as with most current treatments, technology is seen as a false god who will lead to eventual destruction. Many authors warn of putting all our chips on increased technology. The general trend has been to separate man the animal from his technology. Man in the primitive stage is considered natural. Technological man is generally considered "unnatural." Michael Rossman, in another essay in this symposium, points out that man's technology is simply an extension of man himself and should be considered a very natural part of man. When man is viewed in this way, and his technology directed toward his survival, technology may well become the saving grace of mankind. However, when technology is applied primarily toward man's survival, he will lead a much more managed and regulated existence. Action must be taken that will bring man and his environment into accord with ecological principles. The action to be taken must be ecological, but before the ecologist can apply the biological values developed in his laboratory and in the field, he must have input from sociologists, psychologists, economists, and theologians, because most of us admit that man is more than the average animal.

PART TWO

The Wider Human Environment

o

2

ECOLOGICAL RESPONSIBILITY
AND
ECONOMIC JUSTICE*

Norman J. Faramelli

According to ecologists, we are threatened with extinction within fifty years if current pollution trends are allowed to continue. Despite some overstatements by a few "prophets of doom," an increasing number of reasonable people recognize that the ecological problem has reached a crisis stage. All during 1970, leading magazines, newspapers, radio, and TV have announced that we are

*This article was originally printed in the Andover Newton *Quarterly,* Vol. XI, No. 2 (November 1970), pp. 81–93. Reprinted by permission.

entering an "age of ecology."[1] Although its popularity reached a zenith on Earth Day (April 22, 1970), ecology is still much before the public. But despite the widespread rhetoric, the environmental problems are becoming more critical, as the summer smog along the East Coast amply illustrated.

In theory, everyone wants a clean environment. But the real questions are, How serious is the ecology problem in light of our other pressing needs? Who is going to pay for pollution control? With regard to the latter, we must heed the cry of both the ecologist and the economist: "There are no free lunches." Someone will pay for a clean environment! It is the belief of this writer that *ecology is a profoundly serious matter, yet most of the solutions suggested for environmental quality will have, directly or indirectly, adverse effects on the poor and lower income groups.* Hence, economic or distributive justice must become an active component in all ecology debates.

The Lord has entrusted man with the created order; he is to be a responsible steward of God's creation. Although the development of an environmental ethic is essential and long overdue, it should not overlook nor underplay the special role that man (particularly the poor and the oppressed) plays in the Judeo-Christian tradition.[2] Now that an environmental ethic is being shaped, it is imperative that it be in harmony with concerns for economic justice.

THE TWO REVOLUTIONS

In the midst of the burgeoning interest in ecology, a few voices have warned that ecology is becoming a new cop-out, a way to refocus the enthusiasm of the young (especially college students) away from the war, urban problems, and poverty. One can rationalize that the young are frustrated over Vietnam, almost completely alienated from poverty and the ghettos, so ecology buffs are now in vogue. In many ways, ecology is a logical successor to the middle-class concerns of conservation. But that explanation is too simplistic and misses entirely the seriousness of the ecological crisis.

The ecology rage must be understood in light of the two revolutions occurring in our society today. They can be termed the "pre-affluent" and "post-affluent" revolutions. The first is dominated by the poor and the black communities. Their primary focus is on social and economic justice as well as freedom and self-determination. The quest of the powerless and the alienated is primarily for human dignity and the restructuring of power relationships. Many in this revolution, however, want to move beyond "getting a fair piece of the pie" to new life-styles, where "soul" or spontaneity is an essential ingredient. For the alienated youth in the "post-affluent" revolution, however, the emphasis is not on power, but simply on new life-styles. There is a flat rejection of the values of over-consumption, technical efficiency, and adulation of economic growth that has dominated American society.[3] The ecology movement is closely linked with the "post-affluent" revolution. Only those who have been reared in affluent suburbs can rebel against over-consumption and the banality of materialism. It is no surprise that ecologists like Barry Commoner, Lamont Cole, Paul Ehrlich, and Eugene Odum receive their biggest ovations in jammed college auditoriums. The differences between the two movements were vividly expressed by a welfare rights organizer to a group of young ecology radicals. He said: "We will have some problems understanding one another for our welfare mothers want what you are rejecting."[4]

Those who have been involved with urban and poverty problems have often distrusted the "ecology fad." On the other hand, most ecology enthusiasts, and especially the old-line conservationists who are becoming attuned to ecology, almost completely ignore the problems of the ghettos and the poor. Ecology, for them, has more to do with saving a certain marine species than eradicating rats from infested ghetto apartments! To the ghetto resident, air pollution is clearly not at the top of his priority list. As one black community organizer in Chicago said recently: "The one thing I don't look forward to is living in a pollution-free, unjust, and repressive society."

DISTRUST OF THE ECOLOGY MOVEMENT

Distrust of the ecology movement is increasing on all sides. *Time* magazine (August 3, 1970) reports a burgeoning anti-ecology movement. Some critics believe that the environment cannot be as bad as many scientists say. Others sense the profound changes in the industrial system and life-styles that the quest for environmental quality will demand, hence, they are "bugging out" by ignoring the issue. Others believe that the ecology movement has been characterized by too much radical pessimism and alarmism.

The anti-ecology sentiment among the poor, especially the blacks, is still prevalent. For example, one Black Panther leader in Roxbury (Mass.) said: "It is a sick society that can beat and murder black people on the streets, butcher thousands of children in Vietnam, spend billions in arms to destroy mankind, and then come to the conclusion that air pollution is America's number one problem."[5]

Why do the poor distrust the ecology movement? First, a clean environment is not on their priority list, at least not in terms of air and water pollution. The poor are part of a different revolution; their focus is on justice. Also, the ecology groups have almost totally ignored the needs of the poor. Most of the images of environmental quality refer to improved life-styles for suburban dwellers—cleaner air, more trees, better hiking, boating, and swimming facilities, etc. There is almost no emphasis on urban ecology.

Another reason the poor distrust ecology is related to the general mood of the nation symbolized in President Nixon's 1970 State of the Union Message.[6] In a speech replete with many references to the environment, he said: "Restoring nature to its natural state is a cause beyond party and beyond factions. It has become a common cause of all the people of this country." The President also noted that Americans have to make "some very hard decisions" on priorities, which meant: "rejecting pending programs which would benefit some of the people when their net effect would result in price increases for all the people." In other words, urban spending, which benefits the white and black poor, is inflationary!

The lack of any references in the address to black America, the sparse references to poverty and urban blight, and the copious references to "law and order" illustrated the current concerns facing American society. It is not too surprising that many black citizens felt alienated from the President's address, saw in it the omens of repression, and from it deduced that interest in ecology is a "cop-out." To the poor, that was more than an isolated speech; it articulated a growing national mood. Hence, one can understand their charges that, "ecology is a club over our heads; it's a cop-out; it's a middle-class issue."

But will funds actually be diverted from poverty to ecology? As of now, the funds spent on either ecology or poverty are pitifully small. This year the Federal Government approved $800 million for water pollution programs, although far more is needed. Expenditures on poverty are also grossly inadequate. To choose ecology instead of poverty, or vice versa is to make a bad choice. We should not be asked to select between schools and homes for urban dwellers, on the one hand, and a clean environment on the other, while the ABM is expanded, the supersonic transport is developed and Vietnam continues almost untouched by sanity. Despite the deceptive defense department cuts, new weapons systems are still top priority items on the national agenda and devour a substantial part of the federal budget. Today over 60¢ of every federal tax dollar is used to pay off past or current wars or to plan new ones. An apt metaphor to describe the competing concerns of ecology and poverty is two people arguing over the crumbs from a loaf of bread while others run away with the slices! From the standpoint of resources expended, the issue of "ecology as a cop-out on the poor" is largely academic, since both ecology and poverty are being starved. Given the pittances that are now spent on ecology, the "war on pollution" proposed by the Nixon administration will probably be as ineffective as the "war on poverty" was in dealing with the problems of the poor.

Both ecology and poverty have to be seen in light of other national priorities. Dr. George Wiley, executive director of the National Welfare Rights Organization, summarized the problem of national priorities when he spoke at a Harvard teach-in. After acknowledging the seriousness of the ecological crisis, he addressed a challenge to the environmentalists:

> It is going to be necessary to have substantial governmental expenditures for the programs of environmental control . . . That means you will be directly competing with poor people for very scarce government dollars. And if you are not in a position to mount a confrontation with the military-industrial complex, if you are not prepared to join with poor people in saying that the war in Vietnam has got to end, that we've got to stop military imperialism around the world, that we've got to cut out the wasteful military expenditures, quite clearly poor people will pay the cost of your ecology program. . . .[7]

But let us suppose that ecology is taken seriously. Have we properly assessed the impact of the proposed remedies on low-income households? This is necessary from two standpoints: (a) someone has to pay for pollution control and the poor will be asked to pay disproportionately, and (b) some of the remedies proposed to halt pollution, such as curbing economic growth, will have severe repercussions on the poor.

WHO PAYS FOR POLLUTION CONTROL?

The idea posed by *Life* magazine and others that "ecology is everybody's issue" is misleading. There is a widespread illusion that at last we have found a real national issue that is noncontroversial, and hence, we act as if a clean environment can be obtained virtually without cost. If, for example, the managers of a chemical or power plant install expensive pollution control equipment, they can do one of three things to cover expenditures: (1) raise the price of the product, (2) appeal for a government subsidy, or (3) reduce corporate profits.

Capital expenditure in pollution control equipment is basically an investment in nonproductive devices. Given our current accounting procedures, such a venture increases the cost of production. We have for years assumed that disposal of waste into the air or waterways is free! The ecological costs have seldom been calculated, let alone included in the costs of production. To do any of the three items will tend to slow down consumption and attack our cherished sacred cow—an increasing "standard of living." Raising the price of a product will surely reduce the amount that a family can buy. The price increase is tantamount to a sales tax—a regressive form of taxation that hurts the poor most severely when imposed on necessities. Each person will pay the same increased amount per item, but some can pay it easily and others cannot.

The federal subsidy also does not come free of charge, because the taxpayer will ultimately pay it, even if by a progressive income tax. Any tax credits offered to industries for cleaner effluents are really another form of subsidy for pollution control. The third alternative—lowering the corporate profits—seems unlikely, given the power and prestige, and lack of public controls over, large corporations. If profits were somehow substantially reduced, however, industrial expansion would slow down. Of the three alternatives, the first seems to be the most likely. Yet increasing the price of the products will affect the poor most severely, unless we make special allowances or adopt new pricing mechanisms.

In order to have economic justice and ecological sanity, we might have to radically revamp our pricing structures. For instance, we now pay less for additional units of electric power consumption, which means that the tenth electrical appliance is actually cheaper (per kilowatt-hour) to operate than the first. We are enticed into consuming increasing amounts of electric power that result in environmental contamination. In order to preserve a sound environment with economic justice, the basic units of power should be offered at the cheapest possible rates. Then a graduated price scale might be imposed on additional amounts so that the ninth appliance (a freezer?) will be more costly to operate than the first (a refrigerator?). The inversion of the rate structure would discourage profligate use of power.

ECONOMIC GROWTH AND ENVIRONMENTAL DESTRUCTION

An increasing gross national product (GNP) has functioned in American society like a god-concept does in a religious society. In a word, Americans worship economic growth. Yet increased economic growth, which comes about by increased material and power consumption, is always accompanied by increased pollution. Hence, many ecologists and others believe that we must begin to deal with root causes, and not symptoms. And perpetually increasing consumption levels of power and material goods (compounded by the population explosion) are the root causes.

But won't more technology solve the pollution problem? Our perennial faith in the "technical fix" to solve all of our pollution problems is being shattered. That notion naïvely assumes that no matter how badly the side effects of current technology destroy the environment, new technologies will appear that will fully ameliorate the damages. Just as the drug user becomes addicted to heroin, our society has become addicted to the technical fix. Technology, of course, can be useful in developing pollution control devices, but exclusive reliance upon new technologies to extricate us from our follies has not and will not work repeatedly. We produce new problems faster than we solve old ones. In many instances, *initial steps that produced the pollution will have to be stopped.* In fact, sometimes the technical fix creates problems that are more dangerous than the ones it tried to remedy. For example, the detergent used to free the ocean of the oil from the Torrey Canyon wreck did more damage to marine life than the oil spilled!

There is a growing pool of data that shows that increased production will cause increased environmental contamination, even after the best pollution control devices are installed. Our current methods, for instance, extract raw materials from the earth and turn them into products that soon become obsolete. The disposal of these products often presents serious environmental problems. A classic case is that of bauxite ore which is extracted in Latin America and converted into billions of aluminum cans per year. Their disposal presents a fantastic problem since the cans do not decompose. Hence, many of our most secluded wildernesses are strewn with beer cans!

In order to conserve our natural resources, a tax on extracting raw materials needs to be imposed, as well as a tax on the disposal of the product. That is, the real cost of depleting natural resources and the cost of disposing of manufactured products should be included in the costs of production. Obviously, taxing the origin and the end of the production process would make recycling of products a more competitive operation. This would allow us to move to what the economist, Kenneth Boulding, has called the "spaceship earth" society. Boulding believes that the U.S. is now wedded to a "cowboy" economy which knows no limits on natural resources, and has no ecological constraints.[8] A spaceship earth concept is one where the materials are recycled, just as occurs on space flights.

But a massive recycle industry cannot be developed without power consumption and environmental deterioration. Massive recycle industries would allow us to preserve natural resources and help solve the disposal problem, but the second law of thermodynamics cannot be reversed. Any power generating operation has some heat loss, and that is always a form of pollution! So increased recycling cannot be viewed as an unlimited process. Thus, some scientists are calling for a slowdown in economic growth.

Ecologists, who challenge the notion of endless material economic growth, are being joined by a host of others. For instance, former Secretary of Interior Stewart Udall speaks freely of the madness involved in equating the GNP with national well-being. The geologist, Preston Cloud, speaking in Boston to a recent meeting of the American Association for the Advancement of Science, remarked that, "Growth is a Trojan horse, with the diplomatic privileges of a sacred cow." Even the ecology features in *Time* (February 2 and March 2, 1970) noted that the whirling dervish doctrine of perpetual growth should be challenged. The biologist, René Dubos, has commented on the insanity of such a notion as: "Produce more than you consume, so that you can consume more."[9] There is a serious question whether ecological constraints will allow growth to increase indefinitely. Although the idea strikes at the heart of Keynesian economics, it is being espoused by responsible physical, biological, and social scientists who are not ordinarily viewed as "kooks" or "alarmists."

Before proceeding, it should be first specified that not all economic growth results in pollution. Increased sales of pollution control equipment and gains in the "service" sector also increase the GNP. But growth in sectors that cause vast pollution should be restrained. Hence, the issue is not growth or no growth, but what kind of growth.

ECONOMIC GROWTH AND HIGH EMPLOYMENT LEVELS

A cutback in material production would have profound repercussions on the poor and lower-middle-income groups. Those who have doubts about this should observe the rising unemployment which is a result of our current attempt to "cool off" an inflationary economy. (Unemployment rates have already risen from 3.3 percent to over 5 percent.)[10] Also, most industrialized nations finance their poverty programs via incremental economic growth, or a growth dividend.[11] More growth means more jobs for all (especially the poor and lower-middle-income groups) and more public funds available to finance welfare programs (i.e., without further tax increases). In a word, we are addicted to the "trickle down theory," that everyone must receive more if the poor are to receive more. That this theory has not been fully effective in ending poverty is irrelevant; it has worked in part. The poor may not have been helped appreciably by economic growth, but they certainly will suffer acutely if the growth rate declines. This paradox, which can lead to a host of questions about the structural injustices in our economic system, cannot be pursued at this juncture.[12]

These effects on poor and lower-middle-income families are most severe in an automated society. For years there has been a stalemate in the debate, "Does automation produce or reduce jobs?" The experts have argued on both sides of the issue. But from the maze of data some clear trends are discernible. During the Eisenhower years when economic growth was slow, unemployment rates soared (3 percent in 1953 to 5 percent in 1960). From 1962 to 1968 (a period of economic growth) the unemployment rates dropped from 5.6 percent to 3.5 percent. Such statistics led the "pro-automation" experts to say: "See! Automation produces more jobs, as long as economic growth is sustained." But if the ecological problems are as serious as many believe, then that provisional clause "as long as economic growth is sustained" radically alters the debate. For automation always increases productivity (i.e., units produced per man hour). If automation did not, it would be senseless to add new machinery. With a stagnant growth rate and increasing productivity, the logical result must be higher levels of unemployment, as well as a shorter work week.

As our society becomes more industrialized, there is a shift from the "goods" to the "service" sector. As productivity increases (due to automation), more jobs will be available in the service sector. However, reliance upon the service sector to take up all of the economic slack is another myth. With a slow industrial growth rate, the entire economy will slow down. Hence, the problems of unemployment that will result from the slowing down of economic growth, the necessity of an adequate guaranteed annual income for all, and the need for a redistribution of national income, must be included in all serious ecology debates.

The challenges should be clear to us. Although environmental problems are becoming critical, they must be interpreted in light of other problems and priorities. If the cost of pollution control is passed directly on to the consumer on all items, low-income families will be affected disproportionately. If new technologies cannot solve the environmental crisis and a slowdown in material production is demanded, the low-income families will again bear the brunt of it, as more and more of them will join the ranks of the unemployed. In the first instance, new pricing schemes are necessary in order to have ecological sanity and economic justice. In the latter case, we must radically revamp our schemes for the distribution of national wealth and income *or else* ecology will be used as a club over the heads of poor and lower-middle-income families. There are no other alternatives, unless one decides that ecology is not a real problem. The mounting scientific evidence, however, stands as a staunch testimony against those who claim that ecology is a "faddish" and "overrated" issue.

GLOBAL ECOLOGY AND ECONOMIC JUSTICE: THE CHALLENGE TO SOCIAL ETHICS

The ethical implications of the above discussion are obvious— man must be a steward of God's creation at the same time he works for social and economic justice for *all*. We should realize, therefore, that the problems from the outset are not just national but global. Hence, ecology and distributive justice have to be considered in an international context. Unfortunately, the wider global aspects of economic development of poor nations, the gap between the rich and poor nations, the ecological problems associated with full worldwide industrialization, cannot be explored in detail here.

One point, however, should be touched upon, and that is the disproportionate consumption of the earth's resources by Americans. The U.S., with 6 percent of the world's population, now uses roughly 40 percent to 50 percent of the nonrenewable resources utilized each year.[13] In order to sustain our increasing "standard of living," by 1980, with around 5 percent of the world's population, the U.S. will need roughly 55 percent to 70 percent of the nonrenewable resources used each year. Can economic justice be a global reality if this trend continues? Is development of the third world precluded by our need for their raw materials?[14] After all, nonrenewable resources are finite and took billions of years of evolution to reach their current state and hence, should be used sparingly and justly.

Therefore, the current American life-styles should be challenged. Concern for economic justice should lead an affluent American to say: "We must consume less, enjoy it more, and share our abundance with others at home and abroad." To some, that might sound naïve, softheaded, unrealistic, and unpragmatic. Despite name-calling, it may point to a central and essential ecological fact which is consonant with our theological and ethical heritage. In order to attain economic justice, the gap between the rich and the poor must be closed. With modern technology, managerial skills, and capital resources largely concentrated in the hands of industrialized nations, the rich-poor gap is widening. For example, from 1967 to 1969 the per capita income in the U.S. rose from $3,270 to $3,800, an increase of $530. Even discounting for inflation, that increase was about twice that of the entire annual per capita income in Gautemala, which stagnated around $250. Some African and Asian nations are even poorer.

Many believe that it was the Judeo-Christian mandate that man should have dominion (Gen. 1:26) over nature which led to the ecological crisis.[15] Hence, a reformulation of a theology and ethic of nature is necessary. But this should not be done divorced from the notions of distributive justice, especially in the economic realm. And the above statistics clearly point out the need.

A responsible environmental ethic would recognize man's finitude and his place in the cosmos. He has been selected to be a custodian of God's creation and to transform the natural order for human welfare. But he must appreciate the limits of technical transformation. The side effects of all of his actions must be carefully calculated, and appropriate plans made to offset their negative effects. He must further understand that even the positive aspects of his technical transformations affect various people differently. The costs and the benefits of each technical modification are not shared equally, so the question of *who pays the costs and who receives the benefits* is essential. A new environmental ethic would attempt to distribute the costs and benefits justly.

In order to manifest our ethical concerns, four things should be done simultaneously:

1. We should direct citizens to see the root causes of the ecological crisis. The nation must move beyond the anti-pollution fad and deal with causes, not symptoms. The myth that equates increased material prosperity with the "good life" has to be challenged.
2. We should expose and oppose those who would use the current momentum of the ecology movement as the issue of the "silent majority," divorced from the needs of the poor. Rats, congested and dilapidated living spaces, a repressive atmosphere are part of urban ecology. The rat-infested apartment should not receive less ecological emphasis than bird sanctuaries!
3. We should thoroughly investigate the allocation of the costs of pollution control. Often those who receive most of the benefits pay only a small portion of the costs, and vice versa. Passing the cost to the consumer might affect the poor unfairly.
4. We should insure that the consequences of altering the economic growth rate become an integral part of all ecology discussions. A new distribution of income and wealth must be reckoned with.

Yet, we should move beyond the immediate American situation to visions of global ecology. America offers false hopes to many poor nations that they, too, can imitate the American model of development. That model may be extremely difficult to reproduce, and suicidal if it is reproduced. For instance, if the current global population (three billion) consumed at current American levels, the carbon dioxide and carbon monoxide levels would increase by a factor of 250 and sulfur dioxide by a factor of 200. The image of seven billion people in the year 2000 consuming at even higher American levels is horrendous, even with extensive pollution control and recycling industries. There are limits to technology. Presently, America's over-consumption and over-pollution is made possible and sustained because of global injustice.

Can economic justice become a global reality as long as Americans are enamored with an ever increasing "standard of living"? And if the entire world population were able to reach the consumption level of all Americans, would there be enough natural resources to sustain them? Would the resulting global pollution destroy the planetary life support systems? The answers to these questions depend on much scientific and technical data. But science and technology alone cannot provide the entire answer. Fundamentally, these are questions of human value and the human spirit. For example, the identification of increased "standard of living" with psychic well-being and the "good life," so firmly established in the U.S. and industrialized nations, poses a spiritual as well as an economic problem. Theological and ethical reflection must link together ecology and distributive justice and move beyond national to global concerns.

In summary, we could say that the ecological crisis is grave, far more serious than the current publicity indicates. Much of the current debate still focuses on symptoms, not causes. There is still rampant the pious hope that new technologies will save us from the foibles and over-application of old technologies. New and more radical solutions are necessary. But the consequences of the solutions on all segments of society, and the structural changes needed to offset the consequences, must be dealt with. If economic justice for all is not an essential part of the debate, the ecology issue, despite its importance, will inadvertently be used as a club over the heads of the poor and lower-middle-income groups, which include most of black America.

3

FEAR OF DEATH
AND THE NEED
TO ACCUMULATE

John H. Snow

As the ecological crisis makes itself felt more acutely every day, or, rather, makes itself more apparent, more visible, more real, every day, one cannot help wondering why there is so little change in the behavior of men, which is its cause. One gets literally bored at the thought of going through the litany of ecological disasters which have become daily occurrences. Few people who can read or write deny the possibility that life on this planet may very well be a far more fragile phenomenon than anyone other than perhaps the authors of the New Testament had surmised, and that the appetites of men conspiring with their technology are quite possibly doing away with it, and that rather quickly. But nothing changes. Arctic oil, off-shore oil, any kind of oil, is increasingly exploited to be burned in increasingly more complex and hungry machines, making a mess and, finally, a menace of the earth's very atmosphere—when it actually gets through the pipes and into the engines rather than leaking into the ocean and making a mess or menace of the very womb of life itself. The cars multiply; the dumps spill over into the countryside. Babies arrive in hordes to parents who haven't the faintest idea of where to put them, what to feed them, or how to bring them up to survive in a world which will, we are promised, resemble nothing more than a New York subway careening uptown at rush hour.

Everyone knows this, but nothing changes. A few ecology freaks scurry through life with their string bags, eschewing containers, artificially fertilized foods, and God knows what elaborate and continually refined list of ecological no-no's. Kids take to the wilderness in heroic attempts to live purely and naturally in communes, only too often to succumb to infectious mononucleosis or some such other joy of communal living. But nothing really changes in such a way that one can discern a growing inexorable trend of human life back to corporate sanity expressed at least in some sort of shared concern with behaving in such a way as to give the continuing survival of humans on this planet a fighting chance.

One cannot help but ask why. The answer must necessarily be complex, but it is fashionable to become so obsessed with the endless refinement of the answer that what begins as explanation ends with another redefinition of the problem. The intention of this essay, then, is deliberately to be simplistic, not in order to give an answer, but in hopes of providing a handle, something to get hold of, in attempting actually to alter attitudes towards the creation, a first step in turning it all around.

In words of one syllable, the issue may be seen basically as one of greed. People too often, perhaps always, want not only more than they need but in our time more than they can possibly use. This is not a criticism of Fords and Rockefellers and DuPonts, although they most certainly fall in the category of greedy people. It is a statement that all modern men who are in any way successfully tied into the technological net of modern industrial (or post-industrial) societies are greedy. The greed of these men is not so much attitudinal as it is behavioral. They go through greedy motions at best only half aware of what they are doing. The attitudinally greedy man is the one *not* successfully plugged into the technological net but who lives within spitting distance of it. Spitting distance is as good a unit of measurement as any, for those on the outside spit a lot. Justifiable. To quote a black man interviewed on television, "Them white people never talked about ecology 'til it look like they gon' to be a factory 'round here for us Black people to get ourselves jobs in and make enough money to live on 'stead of being help for the white folks and half starvin' to death." It does no good to tell the black man that he is not half starving, but, on the contrary, is living better in every way than three-quarters of the people on this globe. He lives not next door to but in the house of affluence, and he is convinced that it will solve his problem just fine.

The affluent man in America (and for the sheer fun of it we shall describe him as anyone who makes over $12,000) finds affluence a mixed blessing. The plumber who goes down to his air-conditioned yacht at the marina to watch a ball game in peace on his color television, gets caught in traffic on the way and misses the first two innings. The traffic is going to the ball game and from his car he can hear the cheers as the game begins. If he goes into the marina bar for a beer he will hear at least two nautical philosophers state that a boat is a hole in the water into which you pour money. He will nod sadly. His wife hates boats and gets seasick in the bathtub. His kids could care less. He would sell the damned thing except that the depreciation on yachts is somewhat more than on houses, and what was a mistake to begin with would become a hideously expensive mistake if he sold out now. The hell with it. He watches the game and drinks his beer. The boat rubs its fenders gently against the dock. All he needs now is amniotic fluid (the beer will have to do) and he will have returned finally to preconsciousness, the womb. If he regresses any further he will be, simply, dead. But he doesn't understand that. He thinks he has been traveling backward, away from death. For him, this regression is recreation, being born again, or at least that is what he seeks in it. But he does not find what he seeks. He knows even as he sits in his near coma that outside awaits the traffic, the heat, the noise, the trip home to the sohisticated anxieties of family life, number one of which will be his wife's half-disguised rage at the way he spent the afternoon.

The scenario for his homecoming was made standard long ago. He knows every word of it by heart. If he has had enough beer to show it when he gets home, his wife will blow up, and after a few cruel preliminaries she will get to the heart of the matter. She will rise in a crescendo of vituperation to a single killing word—slob. He is, she will say, a lazy slob. He will respond to the lazy because it isn't true. Many times during the year he is steadily working ten or twelve hours a day and weekends besides. He once overheard one of the men who works for him say of him with real admiration, "That man is a plumbing fool." Any working man watching him on the job would know he was watching a master. The beautiful economy of motion, the quick, clever, simple solutions to seemingly complex plumbing problems, the extraordinary mixture of power and dexterity in the hands, the momentum he can convey to a crew of men with hardly the use of a word, carroting with a grin or wink, applying the stick by an appropriate moment of impassive silence, all these things come together to make a kind of beauty and grace celebrated not at all in American life. Lazy he would not accept, but slob—this man so graceful, skilled, focused, and energetic in his work, believes that he is a slob. Watching the vivid ballet of young men on the TV screen, he remembers the power of his own bat, the speed of his own glove, the clean feeling of moving fast without excess weight. But now 240 pounds crush his arches and stretch his clothes. Too much, the doctor says. Heart can't take all that weight and two packs a day besides. At least quit one or the other.

But he has no intention of quitting either one. He found he could quit smoking during the week. So long as he was on the job he didn't miss cigarettes unbearably. It was TV that got to him on the weekends. Two beers and a pro football game got to him every time. To hell with it. He worked hard. He was a big man. He *had* to eat. And the smoking . . . well . . . who wants to live forever. Some fool might drop a Stilson on his head tomorrow.

His wife, good God his wife! You had to know her. She wasn't really that way. He knew she wasn't so much mad as scared, scared about his overweight and his smoking and how much trouble it was for him to talk anymore. She knew he was down in the mouth, but she didn't know what to do. He wondered if she knew that he loved her. The only way he knew to tell her so was to buy her something and what the hell else could he buy her that he hadn't bought her already or she hadn't bought herself. She had her own car and every gadget known to man, and two closets full of clothes. And suddenly it came over him that it was a sad thing for two people who loved each other after twenty-five years of marriage to have only two ways of communicating with each other—fighting or going to bed together.

It was different with the kids. Damned good kids they are. None of these hippies. Both did well in school and went to college and graduated and the boy went in the army and came out a captain and got married and went to work for a big company. The girl got married to one of the smartest guys in her college class. He works for a big company, too. But the plumber wonders how they stand the life. He and his wife went to visit his son and daughter-in-law in Toledo. They lived in a ranch house in a housing development. They had moved every year in three years of marriage, each time to a different part of the country. He went downstairs to look at the plumbing in the ranch house. It was atrocious; actually installed to *give* trouble, keep the fraternity of plumbers busy. His son laughed at him and explained that it only had to last at the most two years. He had asked him what about the next guy. His son said, "Screw the next guy. That's his problem." Why would a Yankee want to live in Toledo anyway? But kids don't think that way anymore. A place is a place. Use and leave it. Like a public toilet in a gas station on Route I. Piss on the seat and throw the towel on the floor. To hell with it.

But moving, what the hell. He had lived in the same town all his life. So what? Most of his friends had left for greener pastures. Greener is right. More dough. He had watched all of the kids in his own kids' high school classes who had anything on the ball leave and go to college and then into something called, invitingly enough, junior management, or marry someone in junior management, or just get the hell out for whatever reason to whatever place. Who could blame them. Every goddamn school superintendent, every principal, every really good teacher, every doctor except the total quacks, in fact, everyone with anything on the ball except people like himself, slobs who couldn't make it through college, moved onwards and upwards. And away.

But once they started moving they seemed to keep moving. It got into their blood. At first they would write you, but after the second or third move you lost touch, except to hear by the grapevine that they were now in San Bernardino and the weather was great after New England. In a funny way it was kind of inhuman—how little they seemed to miss the people they left behind that did them in. Because something did them in. Slowly news of them drifted back —through their parents, or through dumber kids who had been their friends but who had had to stay where they were. It wasn't as if they had moved to a paradise. There seemed to be a special complexity, a sort of unnecessarily exquisite agony to their ways of life you just couldn't live up to back home. To hell with it.

And then something began to come over the plumber which had come over him only once before. He had been five years old and his dog had been run over and as he stood watching the gasping dog lying in the street he saw life leave its eyes and knew beyond argument that all that life could anticipate was ceasing to be. He had gone up to his room and his parents discovered him trembling in his bed. They told him about how his dog was with God, but he could see in their eyes that they were lying, like when they talked about Santa Claus. He knew that they knew that the end of all life was death. He kept on trembling. Finally, in desperation they bought him a bicycle, or a wagon or something which in those depression days would have been regarded as a "big" present. That worked. But as his mind eased away from the abyss he remembered clearly saying to himself, "I am never going to think of that again." And he hadn't thought of that again. He hadn't even thought of it when a buddy of his had died in his arms in World War II. He had felt exactly nothing. He had thought about what to do with the body. The death thing was beating at the inner wall of his skull and hammering at his chest, but he was able to glom a quart of brandy and get plastered and that worked. He stuffed it all back into its cage and forgot it.

But here it was coming on again. Everything could change. You could lose everything. Everything could disappear in a second, like a great black curtain coming down on the whole earth. When you die everything else dies, too. And then there is nothing. He reaches for his beer and sees that his hand is shaking. His sweat ignores the air conditioner. He decides to go up on deck. As he stands on the bow in the hot sun he sees out in the bay an aquaplane, moving across the water at incredible speed, sixty or seventy knots, its twin outboards screaming, an enormous fan of white foam astern, trailed by long wisps of exhaust. Suddenly he wants that boat more than he ever wanted anything in his life before. All that power and beauty and noise and frenzy, God, what a feeling—that surge as she begins to plane and then take her straight out towards the horizon. Straight out. Straight out.

Eric Hoffer maintains somewhere that you can't get enough of that which you don't truly want. What the plumber truly wants is something or someone to make sense out of a life which staggers around the brink of the abyss of death. The man is caught in that terrible ambivalence of terror and attraction in regard to death which is the human condition in the absence of religion. He is also, viewed statistically, an ecological menace. This man with his priestly, Aquarian vocation, the purifier, the bringer of clear water to the community, the purger of waste, is himself an agent of massive pollution and needless consumption.

He and his wife, a unit of two, live in a seven room house with two large automobiles, a tractor mower, a yacht capable of using twenty gallons an hour when it is not sitting in its own oil slick at the dock. The electricity which this family unit requires to get through the week is enough to run a small factory, which in a sense is what it is doing. The plumber has converted his family into a kind of disposal, down which he crams as much of creation as he can get his hands on. The creation, the matter, the stuff of the earth being used up, is, for the most part, being converted into energy of symbols. The possession of this massive reservoir of energy and the accumulation of these symbols are ways by which the plumber is dealing with his repressed fear of dying and death. They are magic tricks by which he attempts to stop time—for time in a non-religious society is simply an attempt to break up the linearity of quantity, seeing life in terms of the waning energy of the body, the person as hardly more than a closed quantum of energy. All physical tasks done for him make the plumber feel one up on time and death. As the electric eye raises the garage door, the plumber feels as if he has gained a minute on death. He only feels this way. He knows better. His doctor has told him he needs more regular exercise. But the myth is stronger than the knowledge. The symbols are closely related to the mythology or, more accurately, the magic of power to spare, substitutionary power which can take the place of one's own limited, mortally limited, physical energy.

Of all these symbols, television and even more, color television, has taken first place, even to the exclusion of the automobile. The function of all these symbols is to create an illusion of control over one's fate. The car gave a feeling of more mastery over the space time dimensions of one's life. Medicine (not its practice so much as its existence as a force in the world with white-coated geniuses laboring away in complicated laboratories to put an end to death once and for all) was another powerful symbol. How powerful it is can be seen by measuring it against the malpractice suits, the sheer numbers of them, in American life.

But television has become chief god in the magical pantheon of technology. Not even McLuhan has noticed the most important thing about TV, which is that you can turn it off. Nothing has so tidied up life since death itself. Who says what lives and what dies, what exists and what doesn't exist, now? The illusion of control has reached its apotheosis. Here again nobody has any illusions about the illusory nature of this control, but watch the rage of a child, or for that matter an adult, when someone strides up to a TV set and without explanation turns off a program he is watching intently. There are, on record, murders triggered by this gesture, and the gesture itself, given the tremendous symbolic power of TV over the lives of many people, is a murderous gesture.

A whole generation of humans evaluates life by what turns it on or off. To be turned off is to have whatever it is that makes existence vivid and meaningful removed, and to be turned on is to be quickened, to be spirited, to, God save us all, come alive. The knob, the push button, the plug, the input—one could free-associate endlessly to any of these, but one cannot help but recollect that the life and death of mighty nations are, in the end, within the highly reduced and focused domain of the push button. The same man who can obliterate the lovely young people disporting themselves in their bikinis among the waves with "a lotta life to live" by pushing one button, can eliminate Russia by pushing another. Anyone who thinks the illusion of control concentrated in these buttons is not a major cause of the American misadventure in Vietnam really, really, needs to have his head examined.

Men beyond mid-life become obsessed with control, and since they have all say as to which way technology will go, they put it almost entirely to the uses of control systems. They are really and primarily concerned with the disintegration of their own bodies, the entropy of their own lives. They want to put on the brakes, stop the clock, keep what they regard as the rot, the decadence, the conspiracy, the fifth column, the "cancer" (or whatever it is they choose to call cancer) from making inroads on the health of the community or nation or world, anything but their own bodies, which are to such a degree their true concerns.

In the simplest possible terms, it seems to be impossible for a religionless society or a society whose religion is empiricism to see change in any other terms than growth or decay. There are no other dimensions of measurement. Where such a society has developed technology, that technology will be put to the uses of quantification or control. Change which takes place outside rationalized systems of control is by definition decay or disintegration or disease, but particularly so if it results in loss—loss of territory, prestige, symbolic possession, influence, power, or control itself. The terror of a quantified society is diminishment. That diminishment is the necessary prelude to new growth, new configurations of love and beauty, is beyond the comprehension of such a society.

Greed then, or what seems to be greed, is reaction to the fear of death, to the belief that entropy has the last word. It is an attempt to create an illusion of growth (as opposed to decay) by the accumulation of matter, and the conversion of matter into energy in the desperate hope that it can be substituted for the limited mortal energy of a man.

"What I want to know," the ecologist asks the theologians, "is why should man live?" He is clearly arranging his own extinction as many other species of life on this planet have done before. Why not let it be? What is so important about man? Why is it so important that as a species he should continue to live? As for all this going back to the soil, living close to mother earth, striking the beautiful balance with our environment which once belonged to the Indians, this is all nonsense. Human life as it is right now is completely dependent on industrial and agricultural technology. The choice has already been made to feed, clothe, and shelter many more people than the earth can normally support. With the continual refinement of the technology we already have we can support this many people many times over, but only by the most massive totalitarian organization, and probably by a great deal of killing, perhaps cold, selective killing, in the process.

But since this is the direction of cost of man's continued survival on this planet, why should he continue to survive? What is so special about him?

This question about the survival of man is important primarily because it is asked at all. There is, of course, no answer for it once it is asked, if by answer is meant some rational explanation of why man is important. It is like asking why gold is so important. If a child asks this question we answer, "Because it is so scarce." If the child shuts up it is no less mystified by the answer. It is by no means obvious that scarcity gives value. Are men less valuable because there are so many of them? Here, immediately the essentially inhuman tendencies of quantification reveal themselves. Fewer men, more things—good! More men, fewer things—bad? That we have objectified man, reified man, to the point that we can speak easily of a human surplus, and question whether he has any special value, simply that we can do these things, suggests that we have come to hold man in contempt, indeed, ourselves in contempt.

But the contempt in which contemporary man holds himself is deceptive in its etiology. It was there long before he began to regard himself as a surplus commodity and has much to do with how he arrived in his technological *cul-de-sac*. The history of man's descent into self-contempt is long and complicated. Suffice it to say that beginning with Anselm's definition of man as "an affront to God" and proceeding through doctrines of man dear to the hearts of the Protestant reformers which dealt with such concepts as total depravity, etc., Christianity veered sharply from its original course as a liberating and man-affirming religion, and became, particularly in Western Europe, the means for a very worldly church to manipulate and organize Western Christendom by the institutionalization of guilt and self-hatred. These institutions remain with us, and it is with their extraordinary capacity to keep men plastic and malleable through self-contempt that this latest generation takes issue. The man who lives in terror of death is the man who believes he deserves to die, who has come to regard death as his just punishment.

Thus afraid to die and utterly unconvinced of his own value in the eyes of God or man, the plumber, like Calvin's elect, must attempt to prove his justification by the accumulation of goods. Goods are a sign of Grace. Death is a punishment, and indeed all loss, all diminishment is a reminder of one's mortality and lack of value.

And so junior and middle management and their families, forced to lose all meaningful human relationships every year or so, their freedom and dignity stripped from them and replaced with an ever increasing salary, become consumers, that is, complementary parts of a growth economy, proving their value (not to God, not even to their neighbor, but to themselves) by the accumulation of ever changing symbolic forms of matter, and by the endless repetition of magical formulas (the electric eye opening the garage door, the turning off and on of the color TV, the purchasing of a car which is "something to believe in").

Thus, in brief, people are devouring or defiling the planet because they believe they deserve to die and see this death as removing all meaning and value from them as persons, driving them to give symbolic value to matter (i.e., the permanent) which can be ascribed to them by their possession of the symbols, in the accumulation and destruction of matter.

But this ". . . Obsession with the cruel problematic . . ." as Martin Buber calls it, is obviously not enough. First of all, it is essential to avoid a problem-solving approach, which is what got us here in the first place. From Anselm's simultaneous solution to the conflicts of God's and William the Conqueror's omnipotence, to Hitler's final solution to the Jewish problem, to America's solution to the Indo-Chinese problem, it becomes clear that massive moral and spiritual issues do not yield to the procrustean formulas of empiricism. We are not going to set up the problem of man's ambivalence towards death and then figure out a rational solution to it, although seen in a certain light, this is precisely what the older leadership of the United States and Russia have been doing with their simulation war games and ABM systems. They have reduced the problem of man's ambivalence towards death to manageable proportions, have, so to speak, put it in the lab and removed it from the vagaries of an uncontrolled environment. They have a solution, too—the only one there is. Remove the cause, namely, man.

It is wise to remember in thinking about these men that people who have no conception of eternal life, of God, of the theological dimension of life, have the gut reaction to death that everything else dies when they die. The closer to death such a man is in time, the greater his sense of diminishment and meaninglessness, the greater his inner rage. Several groups of such men will dominate the most powerful nations of the world for the next decade at least. Their power is such that no revolution will prevail against them; but the situations, many of them ecological situations, which they themselves create will most certainly bring them not so much down as toward a sense of reality, if they can be convinced not to blow us all up in the rage of their constant failures. For it is the bitter fate of these men that they have no other way to measure what they do than by success or failure, accumulation or diminishment, gain or loss, existence or nonexistence (not living or dying). In their fascination with death, that which terrifies them and which they hate most, they must continually play games in which they win, set up reality in simplistic formulas which permit them the illusion of solving, winning, succeeding.

Although God is playful, he is not in the least competitive. He will not play their games. He will ignore them. With God, it's take it or leave it. He doesn't mind if you argue with him and he will on occasion try to explain why things are the way they are, but he will not compete with men. God ignores men when they are competitive. It is essential to know this for people who feel the tug of the religious dimension and instinctively feel the madness of the leadership of the post-industrial nation-states.

In one respect, the ecologist who questions the difference made by humans on this planet is right. There is going to be a lot of killing. There is also going to be a lot of dying. God will ignore the magic of men caught up in the false mythology of technology and consumption. Man will find it more and more difficult to deny his mortality. The material sphere will be less and less convincingly put to this purpose. For a while the poor of the third world will starve and die in increasingly large numbers, as many will be killed as they try to storm the granaries and pleasure domes of the world power structures. Men in the industrial nations who have chosen to extend their consciousness to include the religious-ethical dimension will be persecuted and killed—killed rather than jailed as the leadership of the industrial nations becomes more obsessed with the reification of human life, studying statistics fresh out of the computer stating the relative consumption of food and space between a jailed human unit and a terminated human unit (though there is still the problem of disposal and pollution to be dealt with).

But the massive, meaningless statistical dying will take its toll on morale, and unless technology has established electrical or chemical control of human thought and mood by that time, something which one suspects would cause massive resistance at any point in the future, the whole industrial-technological organization of human life will simply come to an end, like the Tower of Babel. There will be a time of chaos during which man will relearn his mortality and how to live with it, truly live with it.

Moloch will not be overcome until the fear of death is overcome, and with it the fear of loss and diminishment, and none of these things is about to be overcome until the universe appears to be a trustworthy place, at which moment the priorities of human life will utterly reshuffle themselves. A final anecdote may give some hint of what this means.

A married couple, both of them scientists and college professors moved with their infant and four-year-old into a new house. They had built every inch of the house themselves over a period of four years. The house was fully furnished and contained in addition to its furniture a superb library which, in turn, contained a remarkable and irreplaceable collection of professional journals in many languages which was part and parcel of the professional status and excellence of the two scientists.

The wife put the baby down to sleep and set about checking out what was missing, as something is always missing when one moves into a new house. Sure enough, sugar, salt, flour, and a few other staples had not been stocked and she and her husband decided to take the four-year-old and go to the store, leaving the baby sleeping. The four-year-old put up a fuss about leaving the baby, so they picked the baby up, put him in his car bed and off they went. They returned in half an hour to find a hole in the earth where their house had been. Both bottles of gas had exploded, completely destroying the house and everything in it. Nothing was spared destruction. For a moment they stood stunned and then the three of them together remembered their decision to take the baby with them and they began to laugh and dance and roll on the grass. It was, they said afterwards, the happiest moment of their lives. They had taken the baby with them! In a split second they had learned at a very deep level some important things: (a) life is a very fragile thing over which one has very little control, really; (b) a baby is worth more than all the things one can accumulate in a lifetime as well as the fruits of one's own energy, intelligence, and skill; (c) don't ask questions about whether it is important that the human race survive, at least don't ask them of other humans.

The man and his wife, having neglected to insure their house, put a down payment on a used trailer. Their combined salaries made up a considerable sum and they could quickly have started accumulating things, but they made a decision not to. They bought no beds, no chairs, no couches, no tables. They slept on straw mats. He bought one suit with a wash-and-wear shirt and a tie which he wore to teach in. His wife bought the female equivalent. Apart from these ''burger uniforms,'' they had two wash-and-wear pants and two wash-and-wear shirts. They had no washing machine or dryer. During the summer they were basically nomadic with an ancient station wagon, acquired for fifty dollars, and a tent. They would spend the summer in someone's meadow. Their money accumulated at a startling rate. They carefully gave away what they didn't need. Finally, they bought a dilapidated farmhouse with some uncleared land around it. They gardened, kept bees, fixed the house up (they did not ''restore'' it) by patching holes in the roof and making several rooms really quite tight and waterproof. They were musical and spent some money on a chest of viols, a beautiful set of recorders, an excellent piano, and a refined and selective library of baroque ensemble music which they delight in playing *en famille* or with musical friends. They give and take easily and moderately with the planet earth and its denizens, but this is not because they are so intelligent and competent and good-hearted, but because they lost quite literally everything they had while simultaneously discovering that life itself is given and taken away quite apart from all one's competence and attempts to control.

For the human race the lesson will have to be far more traumatic and cruel, but it will be basically the same lesson. Perhaps one of the two children will have to die or one of the two parents, along with the destruction of some horrendous amount of things, before men will rearrange their priorities in such a way as to reflect a universe which is trustworthy to the extent that humans decide to trust it, and him who made it and sustains it and cares what happens to it.

4

MANIPULATIVE MENTALITY: WE DO TO NATURE WHAT WE DO TO PEOPLE*

Norman J. Faramelli

At a meeting of the Massachusetts Welfare Rights Organization and the Boston Area Ecology Action, the Ecology Action group agreed to join the next protest of the welfare mothers and carry signs that read: "The System Does to People What It Does to Nature."[1] Both groups saw striking similarities between the way we treat nature and other people, especially the poor and the powerless. When the Ecology Action group was asked upon what historical precedent they based their slogan, their answer was, "Just look around; it's obvious." Thus the slogan was based more on empirical evidence than historical precedents, for modern technological society appears to be exploitative of both nature and people.

How does one define the manipulative mentality that is prevalent in both the exploitation of nature and people? There are many different metaphors or models one can use. One can speak of the essence or the ontology of manipulation. Or one can utilize theological, poetic, or psychoanalytic categories. In addition, one can employ the language or metaphors from behavioral psychology, sociology, political science, or economics. The many metaphors

---

*The subtitle was selected for contrast only, in full recognition that man is part of the natural order.

have varying degrees of usefulness depending upon the occasion and the level of discourse. In this essay the philosophical roots of manipulation will be looked at first. Then the economic and behavioral metaphors will be utilized. Finally, historical precedents will be explored in order to find instances where the exploitation of nature and people occurred side by side.

PHILOSOPHICAL PERSPECTIVES

Some philosophers of technology believe that the technical mind-set extends to all areas of human endeavor and, hence, we do to nature what we do to people. Consider the views of Jacques Ellul on technology. To Ellul, technology or technique means rational control over *all* of one's environment. "*Technique* is the *totality of methods rationally arrived at and having absolute efficiency* . . . in *every* field of human activity."[2] Technique manipulates; it subordinates the natural and replaces it with the artificial. Technique has no *ends:* it is all *means;* it functions autonomously because it has its own inner dynamic. Obviously, such an ubiquitous definition applies not only to machines, but to all sociopolitical systems and economic structures. It is the same technique (or mind-set) that exploits or subjugates nature and manipulates people. According to Ellul, the problem is not the use of technology nor the political or economic system in which technology is ensconced, but technique itself.[3]

In his book *Propaganda,* Ellul notes that propaganda is the Siamese twin of technology; it is only possible and necessary in an industrial society.[4] Propaganda is more than a series of lies used to change public opinion; it is usually a collection of half-truths used to justify and reinforce the existing order. Thus, propaganda is linked with the systematic manipulation of human thought. But both the government and the citizens need propaganda in a technological society. On the one hand, the government needs popular support "to do its thing." On the other hand, individuals need and demand propaganda. They are burdened by work, taxes, war, and are constantly bombarded by numerous bits of information that do not make any sense. Man in a technological society is alienated and powerless in the face of the technical juggernaut, yet he needs to believe that his life is meaningful. He has to find outlets for his hatreds and anxieties and to justify his actions. Governments and other propaganda sources readily respond to these needs by providing explanatory myths and ideologies. Hence, technological man accepts the propaganda that tells him what to do and what to believe, how and where he can release his inner tensions, and why he is justified in what he does. Thus, given Ellul's understanding of the pervasiveness of technique, the same mentality that exploits the natural environment is at work dehumanizing society.

One can infer similar attitudes in the works of Lewis Mumford, particularly *The Myth of the Machine.*[5] The Assyrians who built palaces for their kings and the Egyptians who constructed pyramids and temples were assembled as megamachines. The slaves who labored, the taskmasters who prodded, and the soldiers who guarded the enterprises were all essential parts. The megamachines used by ancient kings for military purposes all displayed high efficiencies with large-scale engineering activities. But the men involved were truly cogs in a megamachine, or as Mumford said:

> Alike in organization, in mode of work, in rapid tempo of production, and in product, there is no doubt that the machines which built the pyramids and the great temples, and which performed all the great constructive works of "civilization" in other areas and cultures, were true machines. In their basic operations, they collectively performed the equivalent of a whole corps of power shovels, bulldozers, tractors, mechanical saws, and pneumatic drills. . . .[6]

Although natural and technical energy sources have replaced much of man's human efforts, modern man is still ensnarled in a megamachine—the complex and bureaucratized industrial society. In fact, megatechnics has reduced all men to machines. They are rewarded financially only for their machine-like qualities, and are forced to become anonymous, uniform, interchangeable parts in industrial society.

In our deliberations, we have not yet explored the philosophical roots of the manipulative mentality, or as Martin Heidegger is so fond of saying: the essence (*Wesen*) of manipulation.

The works of Heidegger can be useful, as long as we can avoid entanglement in his abstruse categrories. Heidegger begins by affirming that the technical mentality has contributed to man's "forgetfulness of Being."[7] He repeatedly stresses that technology and the essence of technology are not the same. Technology has to do with the fabrication and utilization of tools. The essence of technology, on the other hand, is a challenge (*Herausforderung*), one that prevents things from emerging and disclosing themselves as they truly are. Modern technology challenges and accumulates the energies of nature. Consider the Rhine River, for example, and the building of a power station on it. Hydraulic pressure turns turbine blades that result in electric power. Thus, the Rhine is the essence of the power station. But which Rhine are we speaking of? That which is the source of energy for a power station or the title of a work of art—the Hymn of Hölderlin? The Rhine will always be the river of landscape, yet today it is a commanded *(bestellbar)* object.[8]

According to Heidegger, man challenges reality if he regulates and sets it in order, and thus cuts himself off from the ground of Being. For instance, the forest guard who protects the woods seems to follow the same ways as his grandfather, but he is really commissioned by the lumber industry. His actions are determined by the demand for cellulose or paper pulp, which is used in the newspaper and magazine industries, and ultimately becomes the media for public opinion. Thus, the guard is cut off from the "ground" of the forest.[9]

In Heidegger's understanding of manipulation, the subject first places the object before him as a representation *(Vorstellung),* and then via technology converts it into the product he has ordered *(bestellen).*[10] Reality, instead of being embraced as Being *(Sein),* becomes what man has posited or set forth. Such an approach is based on exact, calculative or analytical thinking *(rechnendes Denken)* which is the zenith of technical rationality. It leaves no room for contemplation or the appreciation of wonder and mystery. It separates subjects from objects and deprives man of the ability to appreciate the disclosures of things and people as they really are. Thus Heidegger calls for a meditative thinking *(besinnliches Denken)* where one can be open to the mystery of Being.[11] While noting the need for technology, Heidegger calls for a liberation from our over-dependency on technical methods and products—a "releasement toward things" *(Gelassenheit zu den Dingen).* He wrote:

Releasement toward things and openness to the mystery [*Offenheit für das Geheimnis*] belong together. They grant us the possibility of dwelling in the world in a totally different way. They promise us a new ground and foundation upon which we can stand and endure in the world of technology without being imperiled by it.[12]

According to Heidegger, de-emphasis upon meditative thinking in our society has perilous consequences for man; thus,

. . . the approaching tide of technological revolution in the atomic age could so captivate, bewitch, dazzle, and beguile man that calculative thinking [*rechnendes Denken*] may someday come to be accepted and practiced *as the only* way of thinking.[13]

The quantitative orientation of our society, in its worship of precise economic indicators such as the GNP, stands as an example of that which Heidegger speaks.

ECONOMIC AND BEHAVIORAL METAPHORS

The above analyses, especially those of Heidegger and Ellul, tend to treat technology as an independent variable. That is precisely their shortcoming. Although technology has its own inner dynamic and values, it is largely conditioned by the social, cultural, political, and economic context in which it operates.[14] I believe that the exploitation of both nature and people is related more to (a) the quest for economic gain and (b) the drives for achievement prevalent in our society than to anything intrinsic to technology or technological methods. It is entirely possible to conceive of democratized and humanized technologies, although they would be different from that to which we have become accustomed.[15] In our society, however, the lust for profits, perpetual expansion and growth, coupled with the desire to succeed, are at the heart of the manipulative mentality. Thus, the language of economics and human behavior can provide useful vehicles for analysis.

Before proceeding, several points should be noted. First, the exploitation of nature and people must be seen as the side-effects or by-products of attaining other goals. Just as one does not set out deliberately to pollute the air and waterways, no one sets out to exploit or dehumanize people. Even the slave owner, unless he was a sadist, saw slaves as a cheap labor pool to be manipulated and used to serve his ends. The dehumanization of the slave was not his primary intent. Hence, there are many stories of benevolent slave masters, who, despite their acts of kindness, still exploited their subjects. Similarly, the corporate executive, who refuses to install pollution control devices, does not refuse because he likes polluted air, but because of economic constraints. (For instance, the same manager usually lives a long distance from the polluting plant, and he probably has a summer home in some wooded or nonpolluted haven.) Nor does he pollute the environment because he has an insidious desire to offend those who live near the plant. If these remarks seem oversimplified and a belaboring of the obvious, they are, nevertheless, ignored in some ecology discussions.

THE QUEST FOR ECONOMIC GAIN

In the production process there are what economists term "economies" and "diseconomies," the main products and the side-effects. The corporation internalizes the economies (the profits from the product) but externalizes the diseconomies (the polluted water and air). That is, "someone else" must take care of the diseconomies, or the environment will suffer the abuse. Given the current accounting procedures, the manufacturer can expel his wastes into the environment "free of charge." Clearly, corporations cannot be toilet-trained as long as they are allowed to expel their excrement into the environment without cost!

Therefore, investment in pollution control devices is an expenditure in nonproductive capital, an expenditure that must be minimized. Given the current market economy, the corporation that is socially responsible and voluntarily installs pollution control devices, while its competition does not, puts itself at an economic disadvantage. The only fair solution is to impose the same constraints on all producers in an industry. Although this is a just measure, the companies will all unite to fight such legislation. For even if *all* companies installed expensive pollution control devices, they would probably *all* have to raise their prices, and such a move could hurt total sales for the entire industry. Hence, corporations exploit nature, and resist pollution controls, because of economics or their perceptions of the economic effects.[16]

The same principle is at work in those who dredge salt marshes and convert them into real estate developments. They pay no cost for the ecological damage done by exploiting our more valuable and productive lands. The strip miners in West Virginia who refuse to restore the landscape after they remove coal, are similar cases in point. To these we could add a host of others who contribute to air, water, land, space, and noise pollution. In most instances, economic gain is incompatible with ecological responsibility.

The same economic preoccupation holds true for the exploitation of people. For instance, it has been a cherished tradition of American industry to move to other locations (or even other countries) to get a less expensive labor pool, and to find areas where trade unions are weakest. (Note, for instance, the movement of the electronics industry to New England, a move which was influenced by both factors.) But does less bargaining power for the workers and lower wages constitute exploitation? Yes! It may not represent the totality of exploitation, but it is certainly an integral part of it. The corporation seeks maximum profits and smooth working operation (no strikes or strike threats) and, of course, this is all done to the greater glory of the free enterprise system. Yet the corporate managers did not set out to hurt or exploit the workers.

One could recite a long list of why "marginal" or exploited people are essential to the lifeblood of the industrial system. For instance, why is there widespread poverty midst an affluent society? Economically, it might be easy to eradicate poverty in the U.S., if we only had the "political will." But why don't we have it? This leads to a questioning of the American social character and its treasured values, something which we shall explore later. But first let us see how a certain level of unemployment benefits industrial interests.

Theoretically, we believe that every able-bodied person should work; yet full employment in the Keynesian sense never meant that everyone should have a job. It means that we should seek the highest level of employment while still curbing inflation. Hence, it is no surprise that most economists regard 1 to 3 percent unemployment as full employment. If everyone had a job there would be a severe labor shortage, and the workers would be able to demand higher wages and possibly initiate a wage/price spiral. But even if the inflationary aspects were curbed, a severe labor shortage means that industries would lose their strong bargaining positions with labor, in addition to their major control in determining wages. Hence, a certain level of unemployment serves a useful function for the industrial system. The existence of the unemployed keeps wages lower.

The working poor also play a useful role in our society. They allow many marginal businesses to continue operation, and where the businesses are not marginal, they make further exploitation possible. In addition, the American emphasis on "work" makes it possible for them to maintain "self-respect," even while receiving subhuman wages. After all, they do not have to join the much despised ranks of those on welfare. Furthermore, it has been said that poverty exists because it has not been profitable to eliminate it. This, too, echoes the American myth: "the way you help poor people is to give money to the rich." It is doubtful whether the problem of poverty can be solved, given our current values and the necessary role poor people play in society. Despite our rhetoric, the existence of ghettos serves the vested financial interests of influential people and institutions.

THE DRIVE FOR ACHIEVEMENT OR SUCCESS

It is much too easy, however, to fall into the trap of economic determinism. In reality people seek more than money. The "success" syndrome, or the desire to achieve, has well-established roots in American culture, although success is often viewed in terms of economics.[17] Yet the desire to achieve or succeed overshadows the quest for money *per se.* And the achievement-success syndrome in our culture leads to the manipulation of both man and nature.

Recent studies in human behavior at the Sloan School of Management at M.I.T. have indicated that those who are successful entrepreneurs or executives do not work primarily for increased salaries or economic gains for their companies. Nor do managers give unswerving loyalty to their organizations, as witnessed by the ease with which they will move from one corporation to another. They are motivated primarily by the desire to achieve, and the economic barometers (personal salaries, corporate profits, and corporate growth) are measurable indicators of their success.[18] David McClelland's work at Harvard tells a similar story. In *The Achieving Society,* McClelland points out that the need for achievement is the principal factor responsible for economic growth. Unless that drive is high in a society, economic development does not take place.[19] In our culture, nothing or no one should stand in the way of success! Since profits, corporate growth, and one's salary increases are the quantitative measures of "success," economic gain and the quest for achievement cannot be totally divorced from one another.

The success drive plays a crucial role in all of American life. American society is based on a winner-loser system; everyone loves a winner. Winning, however, does not only mean getting to the top; it means primarily not staying at the bottom. This was amply illustrated in the movie *They Shoot Horses, Don't They?* The master of ceremonies at the dance marathon reminded the exhausted participants: "You don't have to come in first, but don't come in last. After all, that's the American way." In order for winning to be worthwhile, it must be juxtaposed against the horrors of losing. Thus, I believe that the existence of poverty is necessary to reinforce the images of success. When winning seems banal and vacuous, the winners do not share their substance with the losers, but seek more reinforcement and justification for what they have. That is precisely what is happening in American society today. More and more people are frustrated with the emptiness of affluence, but that does not lead them to share with the poor. On the contrary, oppression and repression of the poor increase daily. Winning must have some value to it; therefore, the plight of the loser must be made more horrid and shameful. Hence, note the fantastic desire of middle America to cut welfare allotment checks in the name of lowering taxes, even when it can be logically demonstrated that most of their taxes are being devoured elsewhere!

The poor in American society are not only considered socially and economically inferior; they are deemed morally inferior as well. They are regarded as subhuman people, who have no right to protest their predicament. If success or winning is a virtue, then failure or losing is a vice. At this juncture, behavioral and economic metaphors become inadequate. Only in theological and ethical categories can one explain the outrage that comes forth from decent middle-class and affluent people when someone speaks of building low-income housing in their community or of raising the allotments for welfare recipients. To provide a decent place to live for a few low-income families does not seem like a politically radical act, but, judging from the reaction it evokes, it seems to attack the heart of the American pysche.[20] To live next to the poor is to be morally contaminated. Similarly, the opposition to welfare increases is much more than resistance to paying a few more tax dollars per year; it is related to aiding and abetting moral delinquency. In American society, the successful are the "elect of God" and the failures are the "eternally damned." Hence, the success syndrome has led to the domination and manipulation of the poor by the rich and the middle-class groups.

But the success syndrome has also played a key role in causing the ecological crisis. In our society the good life is measured in terms of increasing consumption—a perpetually increasing "standard of living." We are constantly involved in a three-pronged process of acquisition, consumption, and disposal which is repeated over and over again. Or as that famed political philosopher, Russell Baker, said: "The American Dream is to turn goods into trash as fast as possible." In American society, the net effect of the process is dis-satisfaction, because that's the way our producer-sovereign society has designed the game. For if consumer demands were satisfied, the process of endless growth and the premises of the market economy would be subverted.

In American society the quest for community and alienation are treated as market problems. If you feel alienated, "go out and buy something"—another polluting car, a summer home on the onetime salt marshes, another unneeded electrical appliance, an additional antique, etc. Our absence of a sense of community coupled with our desire for success leads us to display our worth publicly. We want our neighbors to see what we are worth. And the consumption of goods serves as a useful indicator of success. The quantitative aspects of consumption make it particularly appealing in a competitive so-ciety.

In American culture, personal identity is equated with owner-ship—"I am what I own." Even my virility is conditioned by the automobile I drive, as well as the deodorant, hair tonic, and tooth-paste I use. Through manipulative advertising techniques, we are first aware of the existence of a new product. Then we are made to desire it. Our desires are turned into needs, and suddenly our needs become urgent. We cannot live without that item! We are manipulated because our personal identity is linked with its acquisition. Of course, this is all done in the name of consumer sovereignty, i.e., the companies are only giving the people what they want. But most important, ownership is a visible symbol of our achievement, and "man is what he achieves."[21]

The manipulation of nature and man, which is at the heart of our producer-consumer society, has drastic psychological implications for the masses—particularly the middle class. Erich Fromm writes:

> The passiveness of man in industrial society today is one of his most characteristic and pathological features. He takes in, he wants to be fed, but he does not move, initiate, he does not digest his food, as it were. He does not reacquire in a productive fashion what he inherited, but he amasses it or consumes it. He suffers from a severe systemic deficiency, not too dissimilar to that which one finds in more extreme forms in depressed people. . . . Being passive, he does not relate himself to the world actively and is forced to submit to his idols and their demands. Hence, he feels powerless, lonely, and anxious.[22]

Fromm calls for a change of the current consumption pattern to one that encourages activation and discourages "passivation." The latter is a word that he coined to show that man is not inherently passive, but *is made* passive by present consumption mechanisms.[23]

The feeling of powerlessness plays havoc with the human being in an industrial society, and he is forced to find compensatory actions. He may delight in the destruction of the landscape by a bulldozer because it gives him a vicarious sense of power. He may rejoice at seeing a huge explosion or fire, or watching the collision of two pro football players on Sunday TV. Some psychologists believe that many men are willing to endure horrible traffic jams while driving their 350 horsepower vehicles, because sitting behind the wheel gives them a sense of power and freedom. The violent names and huge horsepower ratings of automobiles may offer many a way to sublimate the frustrations and powerlessness they feel in their jobs. It is ironic that in a society with so much power available, the sense of powerlessness is so pervasive.

In summary, it is the quest for economic gain and achievement or success that leads to the manipulation of both man and nature in contemporary industrial society. But ideological or theological ethical metaphors are needed to help describe and illuminate these phenomena. Furthermore, the metaphors from psychoanalysis must supplement those of behavioral psychology, for man's desire to manipulate may be rooted in his desire to control his life because of his profound fear of death. The above issues, listed in shotgun fashion, are all interrelated, and have many dimensions that we did not explore or even mention. Hence, extensive analysis is urgently needed. Yet there are inherent shortcomings in studying the present situation alone, no matter how varied the metaphors. Perhaps we are too close to it to sort out its myriad meanings. It would be useful, therefore, if the historical precedents of the manipulative mentality could be investigated.

HISTORICAL PRECEDENTS:
AN ANCIENT CHINESE PARADIGM

Are there historical precedents that show the similarities between the manipulation of man and nature? In order to test the hypothesis, "we do to nature what we do to people," I wanted to find an historical situation where those who manipulated nature and society were sharply opposed by those who resented all forms of manipulation of man and nature. The traditional conflict between the Taoists and the Confucianists in ancient China seemed to afford one with that opportunity, and hence, it is worth looking at in some detail.

In the traditional Yin-Yang polarity of ancient Chinese religions, Confucianism represents the masculine, aggressive, or strong side (Yang), while Taoism reflects the feminine, receptive, or weak side (Yin).[24] Confucianism is an ethical system where the ideal is symbolized in the "great man" (Chun tzu). At the heart of Confucianism stands the li, which is the way cosmic harmony is attained, and the way that the relationships between men are structured and ordered.

Confucianism is a humanistic religion based on human efforts and human achievement. Human achievement, however, is not seen in the conquest or domination of nature, but largely in the fulfillment of human relationships. Man regulates his relationships, and thereby structures society. Man always strives for the Jen or Te to be self-realized and mature, to be "manhood-at-his-best"—the Chun tzu.

Taoism is diametrically opposed to Confucianism, as it reflects elements of passivity and weakness. This, of course, does not mean total inaction or a complete lack of power, but should be interpreted in the sense of nonaggression. The word "passivity," as used in Taoism, is quite different from the sterile and dead connotation it has in American society (Fromm). Hence, to avoid confusion, we shall use the term "receptivity" instead of "passivity."

The Taoist views reality in a different perspective from the Confucianist. Rather than worrying about perfecting oneself through one's own efforts, or becoming a *Chun tzu,* the Taoist engages in an intuitive and mystical approach to life. The primary virtue in Taoism is the *wu wei,* which literally means to "act without acting." *Wu wei* could be more aptly called "creative quietude."[25] Man is not inactive, rather, he is acted upon by the Tao and thereby receives the power to act creatively. To be in the *wu wei* means to fall into the rhythm of nature which is ordered by the Tao.[26]

There are several poems in the *Tao Te Ching* (poems 18, 19, and 38) which attack the structured society governed by the *li* of Confucianism. The charges are leveled against the formalism, forced social disciplines, and managed economy of the Confucianists. The social and moral machinations of the Confucianists are seen as the analogue to "the Fall":

> Truly, once the Way is lost,
> There comes then virtue;
> Virtue lost, comes then compassion;
> After that morality;
> And when that's lost, there's etiquette [li],
> The husk of all good faith,
> The rising point of anarchy.[27]

As expected, Taoist naturalism was traditionally opposed to all kinds of machines. Machines exploit the wonders of nature; they tamper with the areas that are reserved for the Tao. The Tao must order the universe; it should not be ordered by the efforts and plans of man.

> As for those who would take the whole world
> To tinker it as they see fit,
> I observe that they never succeed:
> For the world is a sacred vessel

Not made to be altered by man.
The tinker will spoil it;
Usurpers will lose it.[28]

In the Taoist tradition, there is a revealing story told allegedly to Lao-Tzu about Tzu-Kung, a disciple of Confucius. In the course of his travels, Tzu-Kung meets a simple villager irrigating his vegetable garden by lowering himself down into a well and emerging with a pitcher of water. Such a method was slow, laborious, and inefficient. Thus, Tzu-Kung suggested that he use a wooden instrument to scoop up the water. The villager resented the advice and said:

My teacher used to tell me that where there are cunning contrivances there will be cunning behavior and where there is cunning behavior there will be a cunning heart. . . . It's not that I don't know about this invention, but that I should be ashamed to use it.[29]

And such anti-technological strains run through most of the Taoist literature.

It is the genius of China that the two motifs of Confucianism and Taoism existed side by side and mutually influenced each other. In the traditional Yin-Yang polarity, each part is necessary to complement the other—aggressive/receptive, feminine/masculine, weak/strong, etc. The Taoist emphasis on man's relationship with nature has inspired Chinese art, contributed to the lasting Chinese culture, and also influenced many emperors.

Traditional Taoism had a non-manipulative attitude toward both man and nature. It would be useful, therefore, to prove that when the Chinese emperors influenced by Taoism came to power, they not only respected the natural order, but also built a society where human exploitation and oppression were minimized. Unfortunately, I know of no such instances. There are cases, however, where the metaphysical foundations of Taoism were used as a justification for the emperor's arbitrary acts. As emperor, he considered himself beyond good and evil, for one who lives in the Tao is beyond the conventional morality of the Confucianists. After all, life and death, hardships and sufferings, are all part of the rhythm of the Tao. Ironically, the Taoism which opposed war, social manipulation, and political repression was often used as a justification to build totalitarian regimes.[30]

A striking example is the case of the First Universal Emperor, Shih Hwang-Ti (246–221 B.C.E.). Under this emperor, there was a trend toward the standardization of language, centralization, and bureaucratization. In an attempt to destroy the feudal system, he burned the books of Confucius and forbade his teachings in China. Yet it was under this emperor's regime that the Great Wall of China was built to protect the Chinese from the Mongols, a structure which is a classic symbol of the megamachine. That huge fortification was built through forced labor, mostly comprised of the emperor's enemies. It is said that "every stone cost a human life." Shih Hwang-Ti also forced thousands to build roads from his capital to the farthest outposts of the empire in order to link his people together. Their ventures were hardly what the Taoist mystic had in mind when he talked about living in the rhythm of the Tao.

How the first emperor treated nature is uncertain, but he and other emperors used Taoism to support their legalistic and totalitarian regimes. One can justifiably say, "It's not the fault of Taoism if it was corrupted." (After all, there are countless illustrations of cruel Christian rulers!) But history shows that any philosophy that cannot come to grips with structural and power relationships is a good candidate for corruption. Nevertheless, the thesis that leaders influenced by Taoism treat nature and people in a non-exploitative manner cannot be supported, at least not in this instance. Perhaps the real contradiction is that no real Taoist can ever assume the powers of an Oriental emperor! Gaps between beliefs and practice are still seen today in countries such as Japan where the nature religions of Shintoism and Zen Buddhism gave way to the new religion of industrialization. And the new religion is leading Japan to the brink of ecocatastrophe! But the discrepancies between ideals and reality, although widespread, are really beyond the scope of this essay. It does little good to say that the Taoist emperors were "only" human. The widely heralded thesis that man is inherently aggressive and manipulative cannot be substantiated for some primitive tribes. One such group is the California Indians. They appeared to be nonaggressive and non-exploitative in their relationships with both man and nature. In many ways they had characteristics similar to the traditional Taoists. In describing them, Theodora Kroeber wrote:

> The California Indian was . . . an introvert, reserved, contemplative, and philosophical. He lived at ease with the supernatural and the mystical which were pervasive in all aspects of life. He felt no need to differentiate mystical truth from directly evidential or "material" truth, or the supernatural from the natural; one was as manifest as the other within his system of values and perceptions and beliefs. The promoter, the boaster, the aggressor, the egoist, the innovator, would have been looked at askance. The ideal was the man of restraint, dignity, rectitude, he of the Middle Way.[31]

Studies on the Kalahari Bushmen, and other primitive tribes show similar non-manipulative dispositions.[32]

A CONCLUDING NOTE: THE NECESSARY
BALANCE TO THE MANIPULATIVE MENTALITY

In our discussion we have seen that the drives for economic gain and achievement are at the heart of the manipulative mentality, exploiting both man and nature. We have also mentioned that the Taoists and some primitive cultures reflected a non-manipulative approach to both man and nature. Although manipulation is overdone in our society, the intuitive, receptive, and mystical approaches alone are inadequate bases for society. Perhaps it is possible to build a culture along the lines of the Taoists for a small group of people. The California Indian, Kalahari Bushmen, and other groups stand as testimony to the possibility. But with large numbers, there must be an ordering and some manipulating of society. Thus who orders, and the values by which the society is ordered, becomes crucial. The fierce competitive and economic-success-oriented values will always lead to exploitation. A preoccupation with the intuitive, receptive, nonaggressive, and mystical, however, will lead to a power vacuum, as was seen in the case of the Chinese emperors allegedly influenced by Taoism.

Man has been given dominion over nature; he has a unique responsibility in the created order (Gen. 1). But he is to be a responsible steward and custodian of the gifts God has entrusted to him, not a plundering exploiter who seeks only his immediate self-interest. Man has the right to order society, but only while implementing the values of justice, freedom, and self-determination. Unlike other species, he has a responsibility to preserve and transform the natural and

social order. But he must first appreciate the limits of technical transformation with its devastating side-effects, and fully learn to accept
his human finitude. Economic and behavioral metaphors provide
useful ways to analyze the contemporary scene. But new metaphors
and models are needed that can illuminate alternative ways of
behaving and doing economics. Theological and ethical metaphors,
buttressed by the life and physical sciences, should help shape a new
mode of discourse.

A philosophical note similar to Heidegger and Ellul is sounded
today by many ecologists and naturalists. In some way a new kind
of nature mysticism is being born, such as in the works of Ian
McHarg, Loren Eisely and their followers.[33] Their emphasis upon the
reverence for all forms of life stands in sharp contrast to the crass
manipulation of the object by the detached subject. Reverence for
nature may not be necessary, but a healthy respect for the laws of
ecology is imperative. Man is part of the created natural order; *if he
violates nature he violates himself.* We should cease to see the
natural order as something that has to be conquered and subjugated.
And that statement is based more on science than subjective or
aesthetic desires.

An illustration of the manipulative mentality was displayed in a
recent issue of *Petroleum Today*. An article on the Arctic journey of
the U.S.S. *Manhattan* read: "Man has been pitted against his ancient
foe—the Arctic." The Arctic was seen as a detached object to be
conquered. That the Arctic is a basis for the life support system of
the planet, and hence should be treated delicately, was irrelevant to
the author. It is this attitude that needs to be balanced and regulated,
lest the human species commit suicide in the name of "Progress."

The works of Heidegger, Ellul, and the naturalists serve as an
excellent antithesis to the quantitatively oriented technical society,
just as the Taoists were a needed antithesis to the Confuciansists, and
today's "counter culture" is a hopeful antithesis to technocratic
rationality.[34] But no large-scale society can be based on an antitheti-
cal movement that emphasizes only the receptive, the intuitive, and
the mystical. The lasting impact of Taoism on Chinese culture was
due to its coexistence and interaction with Confucianism. The in-
sights of philosophers and the new nature mystics stand as a sharp
and necessary antithesis to an industrial world that has gone mad in

its worship of consumption and economic growth, including its "cult of the measurable." Somehow, the appeal has to be for a balanced mentality and a new set of values where economic gain (and its corollaries of endless growth and consumption), along with the success syndrome, will be given a much lower priority.[35] Only when the receptive, the intuitive, and the mystical stand in a dialectical relationship with the manipulative, can we envision a society with a humanized and non-exploitative technology.

5

TECHNOLOGY AND ECOLOGY:
A DEBATE BOGGED DOWN
IN CONFUSION

Scott I. Paradise

In the recent public debate about ecology, widespread confusion has resulted from a misunderstanding of technology. Beyond a doubt our powerful technologies have produced environmental destruction. But we have mistakenly tended to assume, first, that such destruction was inevitable. Popular slogans like "You can't turn the clock back," or "Anything that can be done, will be done," or "That's the price of progress" have reflected a kind of fatalism that sees mankind as lying in the path of an inexorable technological juggernaut. Second, we have wrongly assumed that while the juggernaut cannot be deflected, it is omnipotent and at the end beneficent. The spectacular achievements of technology in the past decades have lent credence to the claim, "Given time and money we can do anything." Armed with this faith, technological optimists have conjured up visions of great cities floating in mid-ocean, forty billion people living comfortably together on planet earth, and gene manipulation producing a race of supermen. Our third erroneous assumption regarding technology takes for granted the present direction of technological advance and accepts it as the only mode of doing technology. According to this view, technology is monolithic and develops according to its own logic. Technical progress is measured by making things bigger, faster, and more complicated. Anything less than this is abhorred as a stagnation which means decline and defeat for the nation and its people. Discussions of the ecological crisis will continue to bog down in confusion until we correct each of these mistakes about technology.

CULTURAL DETERMINANTS OF TECHNOLOGY

The first assumption, that technology inexorably determines its own development and use, and shapes the culture which cradles it, contains, of course, a half-truth. Technology does modify our environment and influence the framework within which life is lived and decisions are made. But at least in part, technology develops in the way it has through the influence of powerful cultural premises that dominate our society. One of these premises, for instance, has to do with our belief about the place of man in the universe and, in fact, our awareness of ourselves. Far more than some other cultures, ours tends to see man as a species, and ourselves as individuals, as radically distinct from all else in creation. The historian, Lynn White, traces this attitude to the anthropocentric arrogance of Old Testament religion; others might see this as spawned by Descartes' dualism, which judged man alone as capable of thought and animals at best as nothing more than machines. But regardless of why, we tend to think of ourselves as utterly separate from all else and to consider all else as things to be manipulated for our own purposes. To violate nature has become a meaningless notion, since all things are seen as resources to be managed and exploited. Thus the management (and even, perhaps, the exploitation) of human resources emerges as a thoroughly legitimate activity.

Such a doctrine of man as utterly distinct from creation, and the universal exploiter of it, stands in stark contrast to that of some other cultures. An alternative belief, characteristic of some American Indian religions, Buddhist sects, and modern ecologists, stresses man's membership in the natural eco-systems of the planet. His differences with other forms of life are matched by similarities. And it is recognized that the relationships among the elements in these systems are so complex that we can hardly begin to understand the effects of intrusions upon them. The desire to manage and exploit the planet gives way before an eagerness to appreciate and relate to it. To draw forth produce while intruding upon it as little as possible becomes the ideal.

The economic and technological results of these two contrasting positions find their roots deep in philosophy, psychology, and religion.

A second cultural premise that influences our development and use of technology has to do with our beliefs about consumption and well-being. Historically, the obvious need to consume in order to live has brought forth two responses. Our culture has adopted the first of these with a vengeance. If some consumption is good and satisfying, more consumption must be better and bring more satisfaction. Thus we have adopted a philosophy of endlessly increasing consumption in order to endlessly improve human well-being. Curiously, however, our industrial system can only function as long as our massive consumption leaves us so unsatisfied that we are eager to consume still more. Modern technology has given us the means to achieve this goal of increased consumption far beyond the dreams of our fathers and, at points, beyond the capacity of the environment to restore itself. The second response to the question of consumption recognizes that some consumption is necessary, but that our infinite appetites make the quest for satisfaction through consumption a losing game. To consume only as much as necessary and to seek satisfaction not in increasing consumption but in improving the quality of experience becomes the game. This response is recommended not only by holy men of Oriental religions, but also by a central figure in the New Testament.

A third cultural premise influencing our use of technology has to do with our understanding of the relationship of life and work. In an industrial culture, most work probably, and physical labor certainly, is assumed to be unpleasant. Both work and labor are seen as separate from life and as the means to secure the income on which life depends. Since work and production are good only because they produce goods for consumption, laborsaving technology is highly regarded as a means to make more consumption possible. But since our culture promotes an appetite for endlessly increasing consumption, the time saved by laborsaving devices is usually spent in performing more work. The economic system based on these values glories in mass production and mass consumption and for the most part relegates artistic activities and crafts to spare time production of luxuries or knickknacks. In a culture based on such premises about life and work, we can easily find ourselves working harder than we want, at things we don't like to do, in order to afford the sort of existence we don't care to live.

An alternative beckons. But as a people we are yet unable to commit ourselves to the creation of a society in which work is a satisfying and integral part of one's whole life and in which production tends increasingly to turn out things of beauty and usefulness.

THE LIMITS OF THE TECHNOLOGICAL FIX

The second assumption, that through technology we can do anything and its advancement will finally redound to human good, cries out for correction. To begin with, we need a clear sense of the limits of technology's power. Certain things we can never know regardless of the time and money expended on research. These limits are inherent in the finitude of the human mind and the limitations of the most acute senses and most finely engineered instruments. They inhere in the smallness of the atom and the vastness of space. Our knowledge of a solar system several hundred light years away is bound to be fragmentary. Any attempt to solve our population problems by colonizing distant planets must fail in the face of unimaginable distance and prodigious needs for power. Moreover, the power of technology, though great, stands helpless before the intractable and complex political and administrative conflicts of different groups with contradictory interests, values, and goals.

As if these limitations were not enough to clip the wings of technological visionaries, the ambiguity of technological achievement holds us heavily to the ground. Each technological application has a price, as well as benefits. And like a shyster salesman, it lauds its benefits and grants us the favor of paying for them on the installment plan. It asks only so much a month, for an unspecified number of months, and in small print reserves for itself the right to demand higher monthly payments at any time. The benefits of motor transport, DDT, and cheap nuclear power have firmly fixed themselves on our minds. The costs in the form of secondary effects creep in upon us, pointing to possible but delayed planetary tragedy. "Any problem caused by technology can be solved by more technology," we say, revealing our addiction to the technical fix. Accordingly, most programs to meet the ecological crisis offer more applications of more technology as the primary solution. The above considerations place in question the adequacy of these means.

TOWARD A REDEEMED TECHNOLOGY

Although insufficient, technology must nevertheless play a part in rescuing the environment. But the assumption that the sort of technical development stressed in the past century must continue to dominate the scene cripples it in this role. In spite of many exceptions, the public and technologists alike have tended to define technical progress in terms of certain design criteria. These criteria do not constitute a formal creed but, rather, find unquestioned acceptance in our habits and traditions, our marketing strategies, and technical school curriculums. Progress, it has usually been assumed, lies in the construction of bigger, more complicated, and more powerful technical systems. Machines which increasingly save time and labor through greater expenditure of mechanical energy have followed one after another. Successions like turboprop, jet, jumbo jet, SST find familiar parallels in every area of American life. Through the power of this kind of technology we have built our affluent industrial civilization. Its secret has been to massively exploit the stored up capital of the earth's riches. Minerals and fossil fuels represent obvious examples of non-renewable resources tapped by industrial technology. But the introduction of industrial methods into agriculture and fishing seems to some to begin the irreversible depletion of "renewable" resources. According to some calculations, the heavy use of nitrogen fertilizers progressively robs the soil of its natural fertility, perhaps beyond its capacity for unaided renewal. Likewise, the use of pesticides and other chemicals is resulting in oceanic pollution which, together with overfishing, threatens the future of commercial fisheries. Too little is known about the chemistry of the soil and about the ecology of marine life to know how far such fears are justified.

Technology has also been developed so as to extend man's

senses and thinking capacities, as with telephones and computers. Though his senses are extended, man is also shielded from the direct experience of the *natural* world. By spending most of our time within four walls, in heated or air-conditioned rooms, under artificial lights, and riding in mechanical conveyances, we rarely have to sweat, shiver, or walk for hours soaked with rain. Likewise, we rarely watch the stars, feel the dew, or experience muscular fatigue. The trend of technical development produces a massive, integrated, technical environment which permeates every experience of life. Each part depends on other parts, but every part's dependence on the natural systems becomes more and more obscure. In becoming free from organic constraints, we become more dependent on technical systems. Through this process, technology is destroying our natural life-support systems and leaving us both ignorant of and indifferent to what is being destroyed. Taken together, technological progress according to these principles will tend to further destroy rather than restore the environment.

Other design principles suggest themselves which might lead to a new relationship of man and the environment. These principles might be listed to include:

1. *Durability and repairability.* This would replace policies of planned obsolescence with technology designed to last. (Such improvement in quality need not necessarily increase the product's price. A few years ago Daniel Bell calculated that $700 of the price of the average new car went to pay the costs of the annual model change.)

2. *Flexibility.* One machine designed to accomplish a variety of tasks might be less efficient in one sense, but it could be cheaper than several machines and might claim less resources in its manufacture.

3. *Proportionality.* This principle implies that the size, complexity, and destructiveness of a technological application should be appropriate to the benefits received. The power mower bought to trim a twenty by twenty patch of lawn and the two thousand pound car employed to heave a man each day from his bed to his desk are familiar examples of technological overkill. We see a less familiar example in highly industrialized American agriculture. According to one calculation, the number of calories con-

sumed in the form of oil, gas, and coal to furnish farm machinery, transportation, fertilizers, and pesticides to produce a unit of food exceeds the calories contained in the food itself. The observation that the calories consumed in the production of this food come from non-renewable resources in the earth's crust raises questions not only about the proportionality but the efficiency of this method of production.

4. *Modesty.* Some Indian tribes made a practice when traveling of moving so carefully and unobtrusively that as far as possible they left no evidence of their having passed that way. We would not emulate such an extreme. On the other hand, arrogance of many contemporary engineers calls for modification. Vast projects such as the building of the Aswan Dam, the Alaskan oil pipeline, and the super-tanker *Manhattan* are undertaken with something less than extreme caution. The scattering of DDT, mercury, lead, and radioisotopes in the environment make the whole planet a laboratory and all life the guinea pigs. Persuasive advocates press for programs to flood the Amazon River basin, melt the Antarctic ice cap, and dig a sea level canal across the Central American isthmus. The secondary effects of projects like these promise to be massive, unpredictable, and irreversible. A dose of modesty applied as a design principle might reduce the danger of such hubris.

5. *Decentralization.* The trend toward universal interdependence of every aspect of industrial technological society increases the vulnerability, wastefulness, and inhumanity of the whole system. In many situations, for example, windmills instead of gasoline engines to pump water, and production in small local installations instead of big factories, might have advantages.

6. *Sophisticated environmental interface.* Rather than ignoring the peculiarities of a given environment, technology should be developed so as to take them into account and use them. Throughout most of the United States, houses could be built so as to be heated entirely by the sun. The initial higher cost of such a house would be more than compensated for by a saving in fuel costs. In other situations, shrewd design would eliminate the need for air conditioning.

7. *Justice*. A technology for the recycling and reuse of municiple sewage should replace the present sewage treatment technology and thus save our waterways from much pollution from these wastes. If the re-treated sewage was substituted for chemical fertilizers, it could reduce further water pollution as well as the depletion of the fertility of our soil.

Ideas such as these deserve testing and further development for they suggest a new direction for technological advance which carries the possibility of human progress and the preservation of the eco-system.

Clarity about the cultural determinants of technology, its limita-tions, and the needed direction of technological development can dispel much of the confusion clouding current discussions of the ecological crisis. Such clarity will, however, point to the necessity of profound changes in the culture, economics, and politics of industrial societies. Those most knowledgeable about ecology tend to be the most pessimistic about the possibilities of such changes coming about. But one thing is certain: not to recognize the need for such change condemns us to extinction. If the challenge stands sharply before us, at least we have a fighting chance.

6
TECHNOLOGY
AND
SOCIAL RECONSTRUCTION*

Michael Rossman

LIMITS OF THE QUEST

In the Tao, order and disorder embrace and move through all. I see ecology, theology, and technology as more identical than distinct, and think our problems flow from our culture's way of falsely dividing, and the consequent tyranny of the male (Yang) principle.

In the roots of our language, nearest to that place before All divides, "theo-logy" is Knowledge of God, which is to say of the action of order (and disorder) through the world. "Eco-logy" is knowledge of the House, in its order (and disorder)—or equivalently, in the sense of current use, knowledge of the workings of whole systems. At this level, knowledge and its practice are not yet conceived separately; and so "techno-logy" in its root meaning of systematic knowledge, is scarcely distinct from the previous two. They might be used, as in the Industrial Revolution, to indicate the practical arts, collectively, and their science. All subjects collapse into one subject, which has no Name. Open City!

We are used to viewing technology as a path marked by machines, leading up from ax and ax-chipper through TV. But at its

*Copyright © 1971 by Michael Rossman

current summit, we recognize that a computer is just expensive junk hardware without its software component—its programs, and behind these the systems by which people learn to generate them; and programs and systems of the spirit, parallel to those of the mind but mostly unnoticed. From this vantage, we see that any technology exists largely in the mode of its use. In the hands of animals with a different genetic heritage of aggression, the tool of that stone ax would indicate a different technology.

Thus tools draw our attention to the software which operates through them to organize energy. Going on, we recognize that methodical community organizing and psychotherapy are also technologies of energy-organizing—large ones, embracing many minor technologies, some of which employ physical tools. And we arrive back at technology in its root meaning of systematic knowledge in practice.

Machines are intimate extensions of the sensing, computing, and effecting mechanisms of our life-form. The process of our cognition is compounded from experience in these: My infant son began to invent geometry when he discovered his fist and tried to bring it to his mouth. On the third day of hitting himself in the eye with the fist it guided, he recognized that he was not an indivisible point (and solved the problem by moving his eyes one way and his fist another). From such examples, upset stomachs, or yoga, we see that the unit which "thinks" is not the naked brain, but includes at least the body entire. Extended as we are, by other flesh and matter, the physical mechanism which generates the patterns of our thought/consciousness includes all our hearts and all our artifacts (and I think much more). Thus our machinery is integral to our every thought, more deeply than McLuhan argues by citing the way our cognition is shaped by printing press literacy.

So the first thing to say about technology in relation to the reconstruction of our society is this: social reconstruction and the reconstruction of technology are indistinguishable, interpenetrating tasks.

The technology of technology

As we have a technology, industrial chemistry, which tailors molecules, so we have a metatechnology which manufactures our material technologies. These are not in Chaos, some operating one way, some another: they form a systematic practice based upon an ordered gestalt of principles. The technology of our technology is pernicious, witness the sky turning black; but it is first of all *coherent*. I think the key to its coherence lies in the way its organization is everywhere governed by the unbalanced Yang principles of Aggression, Centralization, Isolation, Holding (Grasping), Domination (Exploitation)—principles unhealthy not in themselves, but in their lack of harmony with their complements.

Our culture is Yang-clenched throughout. Changing this is the substance of new politics, whose first directions, I think, are plain: moving toward balance in the Yin principles of Reception, Decentralization, Collectivity, Release, Submission, etc. This is the compact sense or vision which organizes all the notes which follow, about the technological front of change.

Man meets Himself as Machine

Our wedding with machinery is lost in time, and from the first altered all about us in ways which shifted with each new technology. But our consciousness of Machine as *entity,* powerful as a natural force of god, is recent. It always flared up—like newly discovered fire or Cortez' musketry at the Aztecs—when specific technologies sent change cascading through human life. But only when this accelerated to become a steady phenomenon during each man's life, only when each saw many new machines "cause" his society to change before his living eyes, could we recognize the Machine as such, and begin to grasp it as an agency of change.

Similarly, when we yoked the stars into astronomy to use them for planting, the gap between the opening of a science and its elaboration into a practical technology was many lifetimes. Sometime after the Middle Ages the gap shrank within the life of Western man, enabling us to recognize science as connected with technology—as, in fact, a tool which could be deliberately manipulated to change our technological condition. From this point the organized practice of science as we know it begins.

Images arise of Renaissance craftsmen, court-kept scholars, ambitious traders, artifact multiplication. By the sixteenth century our image of the Machine was sufficiently distinct and developed for

Hobbes to articulate in its terms an image of Man and the Social Body. Governance in Western society is still based on Hobbesian principles, its authoritarian control of the spirit patterned after this our first image of the Machine.

During the next two centuries the pace of machine-connected change increased as giant baby Man closed his fingers around his new rattle and shook it. Soon the pace become great enough to force recognition of *progressing technology* as central to our civilization; men were led to speak of the Industrial Revolution. Since then, during the century from Marx to McLuhan, we've begun to explore this recognition and realize how changing technology shapes and is shaped by, for example, our economic processes and our mentation.

In my lifetime, the recognition deepens, to understand ours as the first human culture to be organized around its own continual radical transformation, through being geared into high technology. Already the pace stresses us near our limits, forcing us as a species to change our capacities or get off the trolley, forcing us to confront radical transformation as the underlying and naked condition of the universe. (For this reason the metaphysics of change called Taoism is an appropriate foundation for reconstructing our relationship with our technologies.)

Thus Transformation comes to us in the image of the Machine. And thus we come to clothe the joint-and-pulley skeleton in Hobbes' closet with all the joy and terror we now feel facing the Abyss. But our culture is ill and balks at motion, and our feelings are deeply out of balance. We see the Machine dressed mostly in greed and fear.

We have extended our organization through megamachines beyond the technologies of our material industries. All our functional institutions are of this nature—consider the army, organized medicine, social welfare—all operate as megamachines whose social product is the perpetuation of centralized power. Our educational system is doubly formed around this mechanical image. It is itself organized and operant as a megamachine. And it functions—precisely—to train and acculturate people to role-parts in the social megamachinery. In service of this, systematic knowledge and its practice are divided into their minutest divisions, and these isolated from each other, for the purposes of learning. In concert with this, the architecture, social systems, classroom processes, etc., of the educational system are structured by the principles of isolation/competition/hierarchy/division.

Some millennia ago dominance in our culture shifted from female to male; we've just begun to seek balance. Our image of power—male, overdeveloped, all Yang in its action—determines our view of the machines which empower us, and conditions their uses. We have made minimal use of their softer/decentralizing/Yin potentials. The beginning concern of political movements of our time with sexuality—at present, apparent mainly in the Women's and Gay Liberation movements—opens the first promise of a more harmonious Way with machinery.

In modern capitalist society, the orientation of our armoring has shifted from future to present, and in our searching for security the Ways of Power have grown more subtle and complex. But ego-greed still stirs the pot, moved by fear of the Yin—of diminishment, sharing, release, take your pick. And in our culture of Control, the shape of our technology (as well as the place of our women) is as it was for the Pharaohs. The pyramid Apollo whose capstone soared to poke the she-moon for investigation was the action of megamachine: so many to calculate, so many to weld, etc., each with his powers multiplied mechanically, all working on isolated stones as specialists, coordinated and directed by a centralized intelligence.

To us the Machine is male, and his secret name is Golem. Dividing all, our culture projects what it conceives of as its evil onto the machine, which comes to be seen as an "independent" creation which will rise and turn to destroy us.

Long ago Golem appeared in our nightmares. As our skill with machinery grew, we provided him with hands and a sufficient arsenal, invented in the services of conquest. Out of habit, we are now busy designing his brain. Computers, our highest technological art, are developing mainly within the uses of war and economic exploitation. Now the time for Golem's waking nears, reporters gather at the door with flashbulbs. When he rises from the table his expression will be dreadful, and his two male fists of Violence and Control unbalanced in terrible caricature.

LIMITS OF THE IMAGINATION

Most people concerned with bettering human conditions, let alone those of the earth, recoil with superstitious dread at the prospect of higher technology as a life-furthering Way. Golem haunts us all, in an age whose most spectacular accomplishment is the instant annihilation of cities, in a culture now recognizing that its most innocent technological triumph, Ivory Soap, has poisoned the deepest waters.

Even those who manage excitement about some technology for human good have paralyzed imaginations. They tend to conceive goals and consequences on the most rudimentary levels, in terms of physical satisfaction of physical needs, as if material means affected man mostly materially. Thus among the thoughtful is some common sense that the world might be fed, cities rebuilt, disease prevented, age eased, learning aided, and so on, by wise use of machines. But there is little sense of how changed technology might alter our political behavior, the psychology of our cognition, our spiritual sensitivities, etc. (save insofar as unsatisfied material needs affect these). And a writer like Teilhard de Chardin seems remarkable to us, in expressing a play of the mind that should be commonplace.

But why shouldn't our minds be in a box about technology? All women and most men, especially among intellectuals, are acculturated to take pride in not understanding the technologies they exploit and depend upon. Knowledge of the Machine is conceived of as isolated from other knowledge and irrelevant to most social roles; by our economic processes, it is mystified and confined to certain specialized casts of men. And it is among the technological elite that the restrictive training of the mind on unbalanced male principles is most highly developed. What wonder engineers aren't noted for imagination!

Throughout our culture the natural play of imagination about technology has been specialized and repressed. In the arts, it has been confined until recently to a "low" and minor branch of literature. Science fiction investigates the possible futures of humanity's transformation through its technologies—material and other, from fusion energy through somatic psychotherapy to psi and Buddhism, alone and in multiple combination. Once SF's romances treated ray guns like six-guns; now they consider ethical systems derived from the needs of life in different ecologies, methane-based or machine supported. As its body of speculation grows richer and deeper, we begin to recognize SF's evolution into the signal literature of our self-changing technological society. When we meet Golem, if we survive, we will find that we've heard his poetry already.

People's behavior turns psychotic when they are kept too long from dreaming, a process essential to regulating condition. A society kept from its technological dreaming, from imagining new machineries of food and politics, cannot regulate its transformation, and turns blind deadly.

Science fiction—the speculative extension of technological man in time—has been critical to the present rise of visions with new force among the young. Its impact hasn't been recognized yet. But many of my generation found it a funky precious medium for opening their imaginations—not least, about social reconstruction. It taught us to play with our minds about what man might become and how, in all the Ways of his being. Though periodical circulation of its literature, new content in age-old plots, never went beyond several hundred thousand copies, a remarkable proportion of the shapers and movers of the counterculture—political, artistic, all—grew up reading SF, learning to deal with lasers, the ethics of heart transplant, and the ecological crisis, long before these became official Realities.

*   *   *   *   *

Afterthoughts about technology and imagination

For our repressive systems' maintenance, it is essential that these be divided, save in the service of exploitation. Hence in the social geometry of college campuses, we find the artists and the engineers furthest removed from each other, with the engineers nearer the business majors.

The case of the engineers furnishes the most brilliant example of the function of our educational system as megamachine. When Sputnik went up in '57, scare flared in America. Under this projected symbol the technological race for military supremacy accelerated: in consultation with the Joint Chiefs, Power cranked the wires and demanded, "Give me more of dese 'n some of dose." Triumph of megamachinery—within a decade, how many hundred thousand assorted engineers and Ph.D. physicists? Meanwhile federal support for technological research came to dominate the financial base of university education; man acquired the literal capacity to kill his species; missiles become the dominant industry of the greater Los Angeles area; computer technology flourished in the high-skill spill-over. By 1969 this made-to-order megamachine had multiplied high missilery across the land and sea, and broken man free from earth to touch her sister.

In the Sierra mountains, on Indian ground, by a warm pool blasted in granite and far from all cities, we watched on a tiny videoscreen the turning of the moon's limb, saw it swell to fill our horizon, felt the slow circling fall. As the first man stepped onto moon surface, Karen was throwing the three worn coins of the Ching, an open question. They registered the six Yang lines of the hexagram of primal power—Ch'ien, the pure Creative. The screen flashed through visions of starving choking cities. Torn between joy and despair I thought, those graceless clowns, with their locker-room boys' toys society and poetry of Gee Whiz, they're supposed to represent *me?* I'll be damned! What sad theater that was, its accomplishment so impoverished, with all our dreaming left behind at what should be its flowering celebration.

INTRODUCTION TO DOME-BUILDING:
THE TRANSFORMATION OF PERSONAL CONSCIOUSNESS

Lacking a Grand Plan for the reconstruction of society by pious use of ecologically-sound technology, my fragmentary projections lead outward from my own life. A specialist in technological dreaming might offer weird and unique visions. I have only images drawn from common knowledge, and rooted in personal experience now widely shared.

I write this in the nursery I have just built for the ferns and our son Lorca. Opening out from a wall of our cottage, it is a modified geodesic structure spanning an irregular space, entirely skinned in transparent and tinted plastics, and sheltered by a small bamboo grove. It defines a magical space, an experience of inside outside: its snug twin insulating skins scarcely interrupt the continuity of green life, from grove to planter, over the bed. The two caps forming its airy roof are as light as they look, maybe fifty pounds, and already have held in a gale wind. Their patterns of triangle-pentagon-hexagon, tinted in the yellow, green, and blue chord of bamboo against open sky, form the two wings of the butterfly of Mathematics. Lights and gems will be his hovering eyes, to complete the image for the child in his crib and us as we lie on the floor in meditation. Poor and cramped for space even without a child, we needed it. And joyful energy rises up in me, the payoff from elegance in response to necessity.

Our architecture monotonously develops the cube—only one of the Perfect Forms known to the Pythagoreans and Plato. For them mathematics and theology were configured together. They would not have found strange the notion that living within space generated by other geometrical forms induces changed consciousness—which is what the current testimony of people who use icosahedron-based geodesic as a technology not only of housing, but of psychological and spiritual centering, boils down to.

Conventional building technology is organized around the concentration of stresses and forces, and their treatment by means of brute local strength and gross load-members. Geodesic technology, like a number of other alternates now spreading, differs not only in its mathematical base, but in its essential dependence upon the structural principle of synergy. Its treatment of force is global and flexible, rather than local and rigid. The linear sum of the strengths of its minimal individual components is multiplied many times into the strength and stability of the whole system, which appears only as a dome is brought to completion as a living structure.

Having built normal houses, I can swear that to build on such principles is a radically unfamiliar experience, and changes your consciousness. Even your routine awareness and trivial mistakes are of a new nature—of combination, permutation, and edge-effect. And I can't describe how at completion you're aware of a new form quickening under your hands, coming alive in a style and sense unknown from usual building. But all dome-builders speak of this moment with awe and treat their domes as if they were creatures who could be kept in health or wounded.

Cognition begins in the body's action. Building a dome is a yoga, a stretch of action-road along which consciousness changes. The road's stations are the repeated failures of expectation, and the incremental learning from each. No mystery: the lessons are quite specific. Time and again you design a member or place a prop from a long-accumulating stomach sense of what strength is necessary for support; or cramp your body to lean gingerly on a hub. Each time, your expectations prove to be gross or unnecessary, your anticipations are revealed as fearful. And what guides you shifts, from a grasping for security towards a sense of the delicate power of wholeness.

From our experience in the physical world we derive the metaphors which undergird our understanding of all else. We were raised in a Way which taught us that hierarchies of importance, strong and weak members, were implicit in building. What would the spontaneous politics and social constructions be, of children who played with struts instead of blocks, and early internalized a Way of building in which all components were equally essential and effort evenly distributed, and the power of each dependent on and multiplied by cooperation? Is the social image of a geodesic dome a society without strongmen?

From ecological and economic perspectives, our conventional building technologies are enormously wasteful of materials and human work. Low-skill, synergic construction technology makes radically more possible vision of universal adequate housing in America. Fact, while our cities choke and rot: one year of the military budget could buy materials and land to house 40,000,000 people well in geodesics—and to train and pay the men in military servitude to build them within this period.

Such technology has political dimensions. It invites user design as well as construction, in each way severing dependence upon specialists and weakening involvement and support of the system built about them, the megamachine of the housing industry. Slashed capitalization requirements weaken user control by the economic system. Aesthetically, technically, financially, the living unit thus tends to self-determination. Geodesics are a clear example of technology which empowers people to determine the conditions of their lives.

What do all these abstractions come to, in this time of history?

I am a young man with lover and child and friends now facing the choices that will determine our adult lives, and through them the reconstruction of our society. Low cost, low skill, synergic Housing technology grants us radical mobility. After building the nursery, Karen and I know that we can move anywhere, anytime, and make ourselves a home adequate in space and grace for $2,000 worth of materials and a season's labor; and that a group can move together on such terms and build easily in a way which blends with whatever land receives us. Before this, the straight choice was to be tied to twenty years of payments at a rate which forced one to work at a steady "job," with all that implies. The only option was to build by oneself conventionally, by fragments, while working and renting. Those I know who tried this found the process occupying all of their life's "spare" time for three to five years, and faced any further move reluctantly. So these new technologies free our life decisions from some heavy restraints.

But of course, it's not quite so simple and rosy. Weepy fingers of bamboo hide our nursery dome from the roving search of the city building inspectors. For to live in a dome is to live beyond the Law —literally, since they are legal only out in country not subject to the uniform building codes.

As with Simon Rodias' towers in Watts, the codes and inspectors comprehend neither the driving impulse nor the structural principles that flower into geodesic domes. Designed to guard human life, the codes base their expectations on cubic architecture and stud-&-beam construction, and arbitrarily outlaw the accomplishments of a more efficient technology—and the social consequences of its wide adoption.

It's not simply a matter of being behind the times. The Law is not free to change. Great economic and political interests are vested in keeping the codes as they are. For lumber companies, the codes protect and enforce the profitable waste of the planet's dwindling forests. For the closed, utterly racist plumbers' and electricians' unions, with their $10-per-hour wage scales, the codes outlaw use of the high-efficiency, light, flexible, plastic piping and conduit which now make plumbing and wiring safe, accessible technologies to the handyman. Such relation of Law to the greedy interests of power is general throughout the construction industry, and to the uses of all other major technologies.

The growth of large, dense cities is isomorphic to the development of centralized political control: their populations are more manipulable, psychologically and physically. Now urban population density and authoritarian bureaucracy escalate in runaway feedback, heading for explosion already visible in the progressive breakdown of the physical and social systems of New York City. In such a metastable system, one element of the dynamic is the protection of the technology which both makes the cities possible and dictates their forms, by the political and economic power-systems which flourish within them. Thus the skirmishing between dome-builders and building codes is a perfect example of how the decentralization of power comes into conflict with its organization into centralized forms. For a decentralized, mobile population, which radical housing technologies make possible, does not lend itself to systems of centralized control. Free up the codes! Power to the People!

EXTENDING THE DOME, IN SUFFICIENCY AND SOCIETY

At Black Bear Commune near Mount Shasta, they are building a methane generator for the thirty light homes among the trees. It will take their food and body wastes, and yield them gas for heat, cooking, and light—they don't *like* electrical light—and compost. The technology is adaptable and adequate for a one-family dome. Depending upon the ecology of the location, a more ample energy-independence could come by supplementing this with generators powered by water (as at Black Bear) or wind, by solar cells (expensive but elegant), or by another technology of sun energy, like a steam generator run by a mylar parabolic reflector. Such sources would feed a sophisticated battery storage system—a moderate investment, until the technology involved gets better. But even now such sources tied to a small system of reconditioned auto batteries could supply current for light, the low-drain appliances made possible by sophisticated electronics technology, and occasional heavier power use, like washing machine or soldering iron. Decent steam-generator technology would make heavy-power independence ecologically sound in tended forest land; it is available by dirty tools already, portable and within the reach of group means.

I hope to build a living model of a family-sized dome which will be a literal greenhouse. Inside, the quality of light will be diffuse, the shadows edged with translucent green from the sunlight filtering through steam condensed between two-foot-spaced plastic skins, and through the garden whose moist roots bedded in clear per-forated cradles will inscribe the dome in hydroponic latitudes and longitudes. And at the pole, sunset will gather distilled in the reservoir below the solar still.

Within a large (30') dome's skins there would be some 2,000 square feet of garden, under intensive hydroponic cultivation; poly-ethylene breathing panels on the outer skin to exchange new and used air; water circulated by hand or power, retained within an almost-closed system, making the dome desert suitable (How many gallons of water cycle through a tomato's growth?); nutrient input regulated, from methane generator compost plus chemical supple-ments—supplied by an industry replacing the present life-destroying fertilizer and insecticide industries. No doubt about it, they can be retooled, if production and distribution are freed to follow the people instead of bind them. Such a large dome-system, perhaps extended by a ground-level closed system using special films to trap solar energy for more rapid growth, could, if artfully cultivated, be made to support the people living within it, at least if they were vegetarians. What living in this relation of completion with the rituals of their food might do to their heads can only be imagined.

Myself, I like meat, I want to raise sweet fluffy rabbits and kill them with my bare hands, after their idyllic lives in a closed-system hydroponic pasture.

What makes me squeamish is to buy red slabs wrapped in cellophane at the Stupormarket. With meat-processing as with televi-sion, we try by technology to divorce ourselves from the wheel of life and death. But it goes on, indifferent to our machineries, which may in turn be used indifferently to extend our perceptions or to numb them. *There is choice in the matter.* And I don't believe the alternative to buying a roast of numbness for dinner is to retreat to the purity of stone-ground wheat and stone-age technology.

What is destroying us is not our technology, but the Divisions we use it to extend. We need to be reconnected, not divorced from it, too. A plant has its awareness and spirit, too, like a rabbit: we cannot live save by killing some principle of life. As long as that's true, good refrigeration makes sense. And so does learning how it operates, as part of the process of healing our divisions. One way for us to begin is to get straight with what we eat. Another is to reconnect with our machines as our extensions, and become involved with all aspects of our basic life-support technologies, re-engineering them as necessary in the process.

Many now make such designs. By a variety of technological routes and changes in disposition, the path is being explored toward dwellings which are both adequate and independent as full life-support systems—space, heat, power, water, food, the whole works—and which grace and reintegrate the lives lived within them. Taken together and with a good deal of hustling and, of course, illegally, the technologies now popularly accessible give you or me the power to experiment with a first version of this Way, a light technological power-complex adaptable to home in almost any terrain and sufficiently sunny climate.

Picture domes and other eclectic construction spread out across the land, discrete beneath the oaks, dug in on the prairie, sanctuaries in the badlands. Local materials, local traditions of design, adapted to place and micro-culture. Managed forests tended by plywoods and nth generation plastics, manufactured in forms for consumer use and equitably distributed. Even the present technologies of skin and foam plastics and ferroconcrete are less wasteful than the structural practices of cities.

We have developed one of mankind's most magnificent machineries, the chemical industry, toward high art. Understanding the Ways of chemical form and synthesis, with increasing skill we can tailor molecules to explicit design needs. So far such powerful art has been turned to the cheek of Profit, its chiefest accomplishment the creation of miracle fabrics for shoddy uses. Were profit sufficient, this great tool could equally be turned to creating a wood/cellulose-based industry of plastics, by themselves or systematically biodegradable, whose range of properties would include and extend those of present generation plastics. Who knows, such an industry might sophisticate to drawing its raw materials directly from sun, water, and air—the plants manage, and we are studying their ways.

But within this century, a first version of an ecologically sound and materially liberating Housing industry is easily possible by changing our technological priorities and laws.

If our society felt free to do this, it would also feel free to let the manufacture and distribution of such an industry fall into the natural form of the local plant operating in balance with the resources of a terrain and the uses of the population which operates and is served by it. Such a model points away from centralized control systems and toward a scheme of locally-centralized facilitation of the needs of freedom. For such industry the forms of management are matters of social choice, and the inherent constraints of technology still leave room for many Ways of cooperation more free than those of our control culture.

Involvement of the community in determining the conditions of life begins in satisfaction of basic needs—in shared local decisions about the plastics plant and its relation with local housing. Universal linkage and free access to computer technology can qualitatively change the handling of social data and enable radical democratization of the information upon which decision-making is based. So also can the extending of involvement inward from the plastics plant, perhaps to the point where each citizen's training includes a period of work in local basic support industry and practical learning from early on in such industrial arts, including their mechanical aspects. Outward from the plant, involvement extends to broader coopera-tions of local units, as necessary for a process of basic industrial development/manufacture which in turn makes local sufficiency possible. From such a wide popular base of industrial acquaintance and self-determination, intimately linked by high communications technology, priorities and decisions can evolve through democratic systems, rather than the Yang forms of the economy of profit and ignorance.

TECHNOLOGY AND LEARNING

How degrading it is, and how bewildering sometimes, to deal with technology! The refrigerator dies, I kick it, it stays dead. Hey, the refrigerator's dead! Call the refrigerator man. The man comes, his smile is like an ice tray. I have to summon up all my casualness to ask him how a . . . relay? . . . works, and he's not in a mood to chat. We don't learn anything from each other; our transaction is as bloodless as the brick dinner steak.

They divided our functions early, for the sake of the productive economy in its most convenient organization for profit, megamachine. My sisters learned to invisibly eat their envy at the way my brother and I felt free to experiment with our hands. In high school they offered welding, but I never thought of taking it—nor did anyone I knew who was being prepped for the employment of the mind. Higher education refined their Divisions further. I did my undergraduate work in theoretical physics. Our specialized texts helped us encourage each other to feel ourselves a class distinct from those physics majors interested in the experimental face of the art. So I enjoyed my ignorance of the practical skills of electronics and observation; and they refused to learn the funkier language and notation of the electrical engineers, to whom they in turn felt superior.

Now, each time I successfully mess with the carburetor, diagnose the dog, or rig a transistor device to rip off distance phone calls, I get a surge of the peculiar freeing of energy that comes from transcending the limits, and hence the condition, of my social class. The state is more than one of empowerment: it has a sharply existential edge.

In our organization around the uses of systematic knowledge, material and broader, each technology is divided into its Aspects, and each Aspect assigned to a class of people whose identity it defines and shapes—essence of megamachine. The profile of one's relations with the major technologies, productive and other, determines one's caste uniquely. Acculturated so, to practice an outcaste technological skill opens one to all the social tendencies common to the caste(s) "owning" that skill. (A gross example of the process: you can't get on a motorcycle without experiencing a flood of images from films and advertisements.) From within—in a culture in which men know themselves by what they can do—the effect is of an opening of the identity. What you know about your capacities and potential becomes unknown, and broader. You enter the living state of the Nameless.

Essential to the repression of change is our culture's great mystification about technologies. In our mythology, civilization and its mechanisms—physical and political—are so complex that no one can know many of the technologies which determine his life conditions, or share their practice or control. Each is made mysterious, its power kept from common distribution. Nor is the mystification innocent: it functions in the service of social control. With the physical as with the social technologies, to be ignorant is to be manipulable, and to be unempowered is to be subject to control by outside and greedy forces. Because I don't know how to repair my car and "haven't the time" or the right tools anyway, the auto companies buy laws and the government to guard the waste of production and the earth in deliberate obsolescence.

It is essential to understand that our relationships with technology need not be as fragmentary as our culture has determined them. Anyone can learn to rebuild a car. The principles of the light-bulb, the laser, and the sun are simple and deep, and open to view: God is not secretive. How can I put it, with the resonance of vision in these stiff words? I believe it's possible for each person to comprehend all the essential technologies of his/her life, and, given the means and need, be able to master any in their use. And I think that any large vision of humanity's reintegration through social reconstruction must include this vision of pan-technological literacy and competence, and in fact depends upon it.

What hinges here, on this face of technology, is our image of man. The mystification that the ways of Golem are arcane and difficult, and few are suited to them, stands against the image of man as a creature whose impulse is towards the embracing of All, whose capacities are larger than his tools, and whose future is open. Against the backdrop of our age, this image is not a "rational" one, it requires an act of faith to project. For by the technological mystification, as by the political, your mind is left unable to grasp what has been done to it, or how your imagination has been castrated.

Like the political mystification, the technological one begins to break only through new experience and changed behavior. The walls are thin now and it's possible for many individuals to transcend significant limits of their technological condition. But our culture's mystification will not be broken until each citizen's education is reformed, in content and process, to equip him fully in technology and its appropriate material forms.

At the heart of any new technological politics must lie intimate vision. From what I've seen and experienced, I believe it is possible to raise a child into a new relation with technology, comprehensive, integrated, and harmonious, and that the technology we call techno-logical education can be radically re-created for this. As yet my vision of this is too raw and new to sort out its parameters; I only know such accomplishment must be collective. But its centering icon is for me the image of our son lying on the floor, discovering geome-try with his fist and watching me build above him the butterfly of new geodesic power, while I sing him mantras about Plato and the Perfect Forms.

When I was seven, my mother convinced my father to move out from the urban core toward the edge of country. I grew up in woodsy Fairfax, medium north of San Francisco. At night the deer wandered down from the oaks to eat our tomatoes, so we pickled them green. During schooltime recess, in the freedom bought by my father's riding the growing freeways to work, I went out looking for lizards.

Dad was a Jewish communist quick with his hands and his rational mind, who taught me to turn over rocks to see what was hidden beneath them. He was also a city-boy intellectual who knew from nothing about houses. We bought into an absolute leaky lemon of obsolete sub-code standard construction. And over a decade of work and family hassle, we rebuilt it from top to bottom. As I went to bed I saw him hunched over the midnight dining table, studying the Government pamphlet on how to do electric wiring. And over slow afternoon years helping him I learned to shingle and Sheetrock, plumb and stud, and care for the tools that gave us some power to change things. Then I went off to college, to be groomed for the High Priesthoods of our age: after nuclear physics I did four years' gradu-ate work in the best mathematics department. In the end, all that saved me was the coincidence of historical contradiction breaking open, and the impulses of my upbringing in a humane Marxism.

Looking back, it is obvious and astounding how my experience with Housing shaped my young life and defined the broader House into whose shapes I grew during the critical years from seven to sixteen.

What was imprinted in me was less fragmentary than the practi-cal opening of many skills and deeper than a sense of the necessities of craft. I learned in action that I am a tool-using animal, and that the ways of the Machine are open to learning and use: that I am capable, and thus basically empowered. And the process of my learning was precisely this: I watched and questioned and imitated a person good at learning who himself was learning an ordered set of things newly, in a new context and in response to necessity. It was essential to the depth and way I was affected that he was not a specialist of skilled routine, but an amateur learning newly and rawly, in trial and failure.

The experience also developed my senses of structure, form, and process, more deeply and organically than the schools ever dared attempt. For the rebuilding of a House engages productive energies in grand A-minor cycles of destruction, beginning, ordering, and completion around elemental needs of survival and grace. A grown man now, writing this I recognize how, like anyone, I have come to conceive the task of social reconstruction, the Rebuilding of our House, in terms of the child-metaphors of my most intimate learning, of leading the copper river up from the foundations to flower into light.

I was fortunate to have shared a relatively complete human experience of Transformation in relation to Housing. I wonder how the experience of growing up in a succession of anonymous tract homes produced by unseen hands, or in the dying cities, empty-handed, shapes people's root conceptions of social reconstruction and its possibilities.

My experience with Housing wasn't all harmonious: we carried on our culture's tortured heritage. The women did not share the building save in the customary indirect ways; so my mother hassled with the continual mess of construction and my sisters grew with their hands' powers Mandarin-bound. My parents, for all their politics and warmth, acted out the icon of conflictful Division programmed into our culture: man as provider and doer, whose peace is the action of work; woman as manager of the home unit and environment, whose peace is work's termination and whose standards are shaped—even more than his, perhaps because of her relative technological impotence—by the consumer economy of over-use. Thus even within our family developed the bad politics of a scene in which users are at the mercy of technical specialists and in which the priorities of construction aren't determined by the builders.

Nor were priorities so determined beyond the home: much of our labor to bring things up to code was functionally unnecessary. And even though Dad was a labor journalist who covered the construction trades and well understood the politics of the codes' obsolescence, he never thought seriously of cutting more than a hidden minor corner illegally. In part, his docility came from his unsureness in a still-new sport and the inaccessible investments of capital and time which experiment in it required. But mostly it came from his being in this, as in all ways of his conduct save the political, essentially obedient to the laws and mores of our authoritarian systems, out of fear.

When the impetus of collective political action freed me from the university, it was to pursue learning differently. My experience as a student and young teacher, in and out of the technological orbit, led me to study afresh how people learn what they need, and how to restructure education about this, as essential to social change. Through the lens of this study, looking back only recently over the stuff the tides of poetry bring up and leave on the beaches, I discover this image of how I learned at my old man's hands.

Even flawed, it seems to present an essential icon for the way in which education—the process of learning the full wheel of our technologies, material and other—may be reconceived, as a process of continual regeneration, of beginning again. Its Way is learning to learn by the light of example, of competent learners learning newly. Its medium is growing participation in a shared task, of rich form and completion and metaphorical substance, organized around real needs and broad in its human dimensions. Its working out can begin at any point in human space, our lives, where technology faces upon major needs.

GOLEM,
HIS PEDAL EXTENSIONS

My grandmother always called the automobile "the Machine," with an aptness born in the ethnoculture which named Golem. Surely the car is the problem-child of our day, with all eyes in the suburbs it has reshaped watching its notorious exhaust. There are already too many words about it. But what the hell.

A bicycle extends the foot. A motorcycle extends it more, and extends the eyes, voice, and circulatory/metabolic/respiratory systems as well, along ways modeled more fully by "lower" life-forms. A car extends all these, and extends one as an integral skinned structure also. Cars—planes, trains, etc.—are thus unique in kind as pedal extensions: they have achieved a first degree of completion: they are mobile Houses.

The course of their evolution is already indicated in their popular elaboration into travel homes. As features like skin-centered temperature systems develop, they tend toward primary functional completion. As inertial guidance systems, car stereos, and automatic headlights develop, the mobile extension of the sensory system becomes a primitive extension of the system of memoried intelligence. In war, the mobile House has already developed a step further, present apex Apollo, with its functions under unified control by an independent computer intelligence, directed toward externally programmed goals. From here the step to auto-reproduction is relatively small in kind; and my grandmother's Machine advances on a line of evolution which converges at some distant point with that of the Living Houses genetic technology may create.

One Aspect of a car is thus Mobility; the other is House. As Housing, automotive technology is subject to all the directions of rethinking begun above and others, modified by Mobility.

For us the primary Aspects of House are Protection and Space. Space is many things to us, and our needs and grasping are as intense about it as about material things. In fear of the Void we are driven to want, we strive, we acquire; and in this generate the destruction of our *satisfaction* in acquiring, so that the substance of the object fades and leaves us to want again—not differently, but more. So automobiles are fashioned to fade. And so all our technologies of Space have been governed by a runaway need for privacy—a privacy brutalized in the moment of its achievement by the concomitants of the technologies which make it possible—and I ride invaded by shame I cannot shake off, from the hitchhiker whose eyes and need I refuse to meet.

The shame is for my imbalance, not my need. For our needs for private space, or at least space alone, are a fact as well as a problem, as commune after commune find when unbalanced communal enthusiasm and limited means pack them to choke on the poisons of living too closely together. (Here again it is clear that adequate housing technology is essential to any broad social experimenting with the family group.)

But, throughout our culture our needs for space and things are transformed into our greed for their exclusive control, and the operations of profit organize our industrial technologies unrelentingly around private rather than common uses. Thus the car and its gross undersystem of freeways develop, rather than communal transportation systems. If people could ride pullman compartments on airplanes they would. The engineering to divide cars (or buses) optionally into private quiet compartments is simple, cheap, and need-satisfying. But their design to make any company intrusive is profitable, and floods the bridges with stressed commuters who would rather ride alone before they suffer at the office. Breathing the smog, we complain how technology's killing us.

I keep circling back toward Profit, and why not? In its Aspect of Mobility, the car was engineered around the internal-combustion engine and its poisonous dependence upon dead fuels. We owe that decision to Profit. It is only natural that those who ransack tombs for gold would be careless with the old warnings that we must deal with what comes from the world of the Dead with purifying care.

In the car's early development, external-combustion steam power was as useful as gasoline, in terms of results. Steam machines were simpler of design, more easily user-maintainable, and burned unspecialized fuels more efficiently. For the sake of Profit their development was abandoned. Interests in heavy industry and natural resources, already agglomeratively developed, purchased the government and the popular imagination and forced our priorities to a power-technology more costly in all ways.

Through such perverse progresses we have become dependent upon technologies whose requirements dictate our exploitative relationships with other men and the earth. The domestic politics and foreign politics of Oil furnish a dramatic example.

Whenever the development of technology is guided by and for

the uses of centralized power, rather than of people's full self-determination, the course will be similar.

In giving us the choice of extending our powers, cars make limiting them a matter of choice also. We are not good at this. So we use cars in ways which make walking hard and generate the need for more cars. The ecology of our motion moves in destructive spirals through unbalanced extension. At the center, choking and sedentary, the human body dies with its spirit.

In a communist society with a healthy ecology of transport, a trip by extended motion system would look like this:

	walk		ride			ride car	
HERE ____	BICYCLE EXCHANGE	____		TRAFFIC EXCHANGE	_____		THERE
		(powered, if need be)				(usually as passenger)	

Cars, communalized to match the customs, would reside at the traffic exchanges. Around these would extend neighborhood sytems of bikes—redesigned to accommodate multiple riders, babies, packages, etc.—and their thoroughfares, terminating in the block bike-rack, unlocked. The operation and distribution of bikes, cars, and their stations would be designed to satisfy not only local mobility needs, but the needs of health of the bodies using them. And custom would follow ecological suit. One's average daily minimum requirements of cycling (or equivalent muscle activity) would be a matter of common knowledge and practice; and the spacing of houses, stores, and car stations would in turn be designed around it.

Such a technology of person-transport would revolutionize short travel: the materials/energy it consumes could be reduced by a factor of ten. New habits plus re-engineered power could do the same for long travel. In neither case would our personal capacities be diminished in any way. Only our habits make technology wasting.

GOLEM,
HIS LOWER NERVOUS SYSTEM

A higher form of public utility than transportation is the telephone, which extends the nervous system through the ear and by its electric web links us into a common, highly decentralized body. By its nature, the phone network demands construction and operation as a whole, unified around local requirements. Once such a network is established, distance essentially vanishes as a factor in communication through it, and the real cost of any call depends mainly on time. Thus this technology's natural social embedding is as a free-access network maintained by the State, or in an unsocialized economy by a uniform time-use tax.

Here we have nothing of the sort: access is not a function of need, and accumulated power enjoys more of the system's benefits at a sharply preferential rate. Economically and politically, this technology is regulated by the Government for private profit. The social contradictions inherent in this scheme are so blatant that no corporate body in America is so universally hated as the phone company. Thus its "property" meets the people in an interface of theft. The very codes which give business and other powers access to the network's more highly organized potentials are easily stolen, liberated for general access. As it becomes more sophisticated, the power of phone technology will become even less guardable, given sufficient technical knowledge among the people at large. (Even a visually transmitted thumbprint access code could be ripped off and spread around by photograph or videotape.)

If the Government didn't outlaw free use of technology, the contradictions maintained by private power would be unprotected and would diminish by our cooperation.

The phone company charges $2500 a month for one full-time, America-wide, free-access (WATS) line. Installed in a room in your town and fully used, people could call anywhere for $3.40 per hour. (Bell's cheapest general night distance is $20 per hour.) With four lines in a downtown room, hooked into a black box ($100 worth of circuitry) and an operator, you could phone in and speak in conference with people in four other cities, for $15 per hour. (Bell charges $100 per hour.) With a $10 pickup/amplifier attached to each phone, five *groups* in separate cities could speak together for this hourly rate—if Uncle Sam and Ma Bell would let them.

What this example implies must be understood in the light of the conversion of phone technology to videophone, not a decade away. This fuller medium—extending the eye, our principal information sense—will be as accessible to simple public invention (and doubtless as thoroughly guarded from it). Your downtown people's video-phone ripoff office would have a gentle room with cushions, tea, and four wall-sized video screens. After the capital of its creation, any sixty (say) people in any five cities could meet together in life-sized live electronic image, for that total price of $15/hr. multiplied by a factor R best thought of as a ratio:

$$R = \frac{\text{future cost of common local videophone call}}{\text{present cost of common local phone call}}$$

After the amortization of system conversion and the higher system operating costs stabilize—i.e., within two decades—and disregarding inflation, I should think R will be less than two. That is, the meeting could come off for 50¢ per person per hour.

Brought within common means, such a revolutionarily adequate technology of group communications has radical implications for the forms of political, social, and economic organization which depend upon group cooperation. Roughly speaking, if such technology extends fully to the neighborhood level, these forms of our organizing become distance independent. (This condition is precisely achieved when any person or group has refusable access to any other through unrestricted use of a *vivid* communications system—that is, one in which transmitted sense impressions cannot be distinguished from present ones by the unaided senses. Vividness in eye and ear is achievable by extension of present technologies; the other senses will require new means, presently conceivable.)

We are still at the mercy of physical distance, which forces us to abstract our broader relationships and conduct them through centralized intermediating agencies. The authoritarian forms of our educational system and our political agencies reflect this equally. To the extent that a communications technology is vivid, ample, free, and distance-canceling, it is an essential technology for enabling the democratic socialization of decision-making and learning processes. In this is reflected its nature as a collective nervous extension. And the fuller glory of our development along this technological line will be realized only as through it our politics, our learning, our industrial invention, etc., are transformed into fully decentralized and self-determined processes.

Even in their present crippled forms, radio and television are instrumental in the ecology of our transformation towards distance-independent social organization. The televised impact of the early southern Civil Rights events was vital to the appearance of the New Left. For a slower example: these media's economies find convenient our division and segregation along lines of age, ethnic group, productive class, and so on; which accounts for the (airway) ghettoized audiences of the radio dial and TV program. Now, as talk-back radio appears its energies revolve around political matters, as does the hiring/firing of its jockeys. San Francisco now moves to mount video cameras at neighborhood location. Their first use would be to coordinate town meetings with city government through the community-supported educational TV station. In such ways is expressed the straining within us for decentralized forms of political involvement and the patterns of communication which support them, as these open through technology.

GOLEM,
HIS HIGHER NERVOUS SYSTEM

How Form moves within us: I recognize now that what has moved in me, what I have been developing on this note-road from House to Mobility to Communications, is a vision of Golem as (Hu)-Man, of our technology and society as organized in our image. As, of course, they are, being our extension. But what drives my vision is the understanding that this image is not only mutating, but is deliberately mutable. The deeper name of our species is *Homo Proteus,* and megamechanical man is only one of our possible Forms.

We can lay hold of our Being in any of its Aspects to begin transformation. Few people believe this now about the Mechanical Aspect. These days the works of the Machine express uglinesses so great that we cry out to deny the responsibility, to deny that their image is ours. Even most of the most humane are misled to phrase the struggle as Man against Machine. In this as many other ways, we express the deep feeling of impotence that bounds most of our condition, and shapes the gut belief that nothing can be done. McLuhanism likewise views us as relatively helpless in the hands of Golem, carried through preordained transformations by each new device.

Well, I say it again: the images of man, his society, and his technology interpenetrate, change similtaneously. Machines should be no more mystifying than our mirrors, and whatever power we have to change our image is reflected equally in them. A different image of Golem is possible, and beckons in our current transformation along the lines of self-determination and reconnection to the organic World. Golem as Megamachine, the primitive, literal extension of the human body, reflects the image of the Social Body articulated in hierarchical class society. This key metaphor, centering around an individual ego inside its body House, organizes our culture now. It is in the initial death throes of being replaced by a new organizing metaphor. The new metaphor may describe the essential entity "man" as a many-equal-personed body uniting by communication into one collective consciousness. Or, with luck and choice, it may be more subtle in its harmony, balancing the Aspects of consciousness, individual and collective.

Change begins in the mind, which, for Golem as for us, includes the higher nervous sytem. Computers, which extend some of our functions of intelligence, are our most marvelous technology, and the one most awesome in its potential for our change. It opens new dimensions for the collectivization of consciousness (and for individuation as well), with radical implications for our distant evolution and our immediate politics. For by computer technology we extend intelligent consciousness in a projected form which can be operated upon, and deliberately transformed, by all the gathered skills and knowledge of our persons and culture. More clearly than our attempt to reconstruct our genetic heritage of aggression, our evolution of computers displays us as the species *Homo Proteus.*

Some of my friends have formed an electronics/design company leading toward a goal of marketing a home computer bank, tied to large central facilities, for the price of a new car. Others have worked on first generation bootstrapping programs designed for self-learning of the skills of using computers as creative extensions.

In your home, the extension of a system which can connect you vividly with anyone and which gives you free access to all mankind's recorded knowledge, visual and aural, all record of all work in progress; all the day's news and the opinions of any who care to offer, in summary or total detail; all the programmable knowledge processes of our civilization. In short, universal immediate access to all of our culture's information—the fundamental basis both for collec- tivization of consciousness and for the full potentials of individuation. And with and beyond this, the mechanical empowerment of per- sonal/group consciousness, by the enormous multiplication of its lower ("mechanical") powers. Only the poetry of science fiction has attempted to survey the consequences, and it has been most notably deficient in attending to politics and sex.

I mean, what will you do with your extension when you get it, how will you play? Learn to build a solar generator, order the parts, and ask someone to show you how to solder? Get a weekly grocery list keyed to cheapest solutions for your nutrition and taste, that tells you what to buy where, when? Complete its integration into your House so that it turns off unused lights and regulates the entire House metabolism? Work with five others somewhere to make and spread a videotape on government pollution, drawing on public input of muckraking videotapers who go out fresh each day in every city to follow leads? Have available to your isolated commune most of the culture's light technological resources? Research chemicals and their precautions, and compute the ideal time for simultaneous demolition of Doggy Diners by a hundred highways?

Think fast. Given your socioeconomic class of habits, by 1984 you'll be linked into a first-generation system with these capacities. How timid, naïve, unimaginative our uses will be at first! But go to the poets, they know.

Computers make possible a technology of vivid direct person- to-person communication and universal information access, *assisted* rather than regulated by semicentralized agencies which operate to refine its fidelity and connectivity, and to extend the depth of its memory and low reasoning powers. The tendency of their free use is to render communication utterly decentralized.

Consider the re-formation of our systems learning through such a technology. Lacking adequate positive icons, its depth is best ex- pressed negatively. All material need for the present centralized structures of education—of power, physical plant, department and discipline, management, whatever—would vanish, and with it the restrictive power to enforce them. Even within our present disgusting customs, Martha could start study at age seven or forty-seven via her home terminal and under the tutelage of Chemist X (who would probably bill her), and in her time and way qualify through company knowledge tests and his endorsement for employment with Dow Chemical, meanwhile practicing Tai Chi on Wednesdays with a master in Arizona. Damn! what will become of the classroom, the administration, professionalism, fund raising, face saving, and the uniform curriculum? What will they do with all those empty buildings?

We should see instead a wild flowering of depth experiment in the forms and processes of small group interaction, which forms the social foundation of learning. For the foundation of material limitation on which depends the present authoritarian and fragmenting character of our educational system will largely disappear.

All this describes equally the transformation of our systems of politics and governance, by radically decentralized forms and processes.

In particular, for the first time a full popular democracy becomes possible. Hitherto our technological limitations in the handling of distance and social information made democracy necessarily *representative* in any group of people too large to be spoken to with the unaided voice. (For this reason all such government of groups has been, in a slightly broader sense, representative—for equally in fact, if not in superficial will, do people render up their power to a central agency, in the Athenian polis or an army squad.) From this hierarchical imperative follows the centralization of democracy and its present universal organization in forms of soft authoritarian control.

High computer/communications technology makes possible the abolition of representative government and the institution of simple, direct popular-democratic government, the full realization of the classic process: a problem is recognized, the people become informed through study, conference, debate, and then decide what to do. A rough sketch: By an open "signaling" process, problems of local or broader scope are called to formal community attention; an initial instant mass straw vote defines their urgency. You decide how much time/energy you want to put in on this one, for starters, and compute a learning program which will fill this best—perhaps drawing advice from the public market of political-decision-learning programmers. At the console, you read, see, and talk with whom you wish; extend/deepen your search if you choose. When you are ready to decide, you register; when enough register, a final date is set; on it the votes announce themselves to you; after that, the process of implementation begins. By 1984, America could govern itself by a system of totally decentralized authority and semicentralized agency, in which every person who wanted to share directly in any given public decision would be totally enfranchised and enabled to do so—a system of maximal political self-determination.

What the actual evolution of small and large group governance will be, given such a free-access system to grow with, we can only speculate. The system is rapidly coming into existence as computers learn to read and generate programs directing the hooking together of their memory banks and operations, in the early stages of evolution towards fully conscious, self-directed life; and as blind and greedy economic processes contrive to fit our fingers to their keys. Surely the struggle central to the system's human use—and to human life itself, likely—will be around the repressive regulation of this intelligence, the authoritarian control of its access and use. In this struggle, freedom leads us towards full symbiosis with Golem as he matures; I think that repression leads to death at his hands, and ours within them.

The demystification of technology, the propagation of knowledge and means for its use at the popular level—all ripely inherent in free use of computer technology—are essential strategies of struggle against repressive centralized power and are key to the democratization of technological society.

GOLEM,
HIS TALENT

We are left with the basic question of our relationship with the means of production. Let me deal with the management of material production by an example on the highest industrial level.

I wanted to adapt my phone to full-room use. I went down to the local Radio Shack outlet and bought a kit, with a printed program of assembly which said some things about the subtle magic of transistors. The kit held components, simple like wire and sophisticated like transformers. From raw materials onward, most of the process which produced, assembled, and distributed the components was done by a semi-integrated complex of machinery involving relatively little human labor or supervision—a process which, in a greedy way, begins even to take account automatically of my needs and changing desires.

If we reach Year 2000, when my son will be my age, his computer will help him decide to add new circuitry to it, help him do and understand this, and help him coordinate the mechanics of component-arrival for local pickup. The components will be sophisticated versions of the minimal-material/high-skill integrated microcircuitry which even now is reducing the human labor of electronic technology by a factor of ten, from production through assembly. They will be manufactured by completely cybernated/automated machinery with highly flexible output. The scarce-material input to this plant will be mostly reclaimed, for electronic technology lends itself to this and its uses won't be wasteful; its other raw materials will be drawn from regenerative natural sources. Its energy will derive from tidal or deep-buried atomic sources, and the dispersal of its wastes will be integrated with the ecology. The machinery will be inhabited by men and women who help the pilgrim young to understand its workings and complete its capacities for self-repair. They will view the machine as their extension and not themselves as its, as is the custom now.

No human labor will be wasted in routine decisions about component production, provided these be made naturally, for common benefit and not for private profit—my son's order, habits, and expectations will be integrated automatically with everyone's, and production flexibly tailored to this; or a message returned to revise these in view of production's limits. Human creation which augments the system's capacities along its determined priorities will feed in and be implemented as a matter of course.

When decisions about the system's priorities must be centralized in *time,* rather than continuously determined by the feedback of people's changing uses, notice of this will flow to the population affected by such decisions. (In a free information system, the necessity of decisions cannot be disguised.) As with governance in general, full choice-information will be available, and those who wish to share decision will be empowered to decide such matters as whether production should be organized around a different rare metal for

ecological reasons, or re-engineered around a breakthrough minia-
turization technology, or used to facilitate youth involvement in the
use of personal weaponry.

This is a prototype sketch of the full collectivization of the
management and use of the electronics/computer industry. The de-
tails of ownership remain—as with telephones, such technology
opens in harmony with common ownership. Every other industrial
technology is now becoming capable of such re-engineering toward
cyber-integrated, automated production and full shared control. The
technology of our technologies, the industry of generating these
industries and their plants, is itself susceptible to this transformation.

Thus the control and decision processes of material production
become fully automated in their lower reaches, are decentralized in
space and time, and absorbed invisibly into the natural processes of
daily use guided by self-determined learning and goals. In their higher
reaches, as with politics, universal empowerment in the mechanical
aspects of decision-making becomes possible—for example, a crude
technology of forecast of the implications of decisions will soon be
universally available through computers (at least to those who can
pay for it).

In centrally cybernated production, as with our present industry,
gross material accumulations may still be necessary to the freeing of
human labor. But the accumulation of persons this now entails will
be sharply reduced, and retechnologized communication will make
unnecessary the centralization of decision-power which has always
accompanied such accumulation.

ON GRACE AND WASTE

The exploitative economy seems to condemn us to destructive
cycles of use. We have come to look upon these as inherent in our
technologies: to believe, e.g., that ecological destruction is the inevitable concomitant of any massive dependence upon progressive
industry, or that analysis is the death of the spirit. I have said nothing
against this belief so far. In sketching a social reconstruction un-
ashamedly ample in its use of low and high technologies, apart from
banishing smog by steam, I've ignored the question of how we deal
with the mess of our uses. Nor am I fixated on the common night-

mare future wherein we sit with shriveled legs, helpless as eggs, in vehicles which giant brains guide to work. In their service, we are employed as components handling minute fractions of complex tasks whose ramifications we can't possibly comprehend or control. Just to make sure, Big Brother watches our every motion through Golem's omnipotent eyes.

Well, we all see technology as our projection, that's not just an intellectual's inkling. Those who believe that its furtherance is inevitably authoritarian or messy are hypnotized by a few of their Aspects in its mirror, and deep in the spirit do not believe we can change. Here again, we come to our core conception of Man as a being and species.

I believe instead that the furthering potential and grace of our material technology is to do more with less. This grace is the grace of Mathematics, our inner language of the material world. As the world is our well for Metaphor, whose unfleshed bones are the body of Mathematics, this is the grace of Metaphor as well. And as Metaphor is fleshed into social forms, this grace reappears as the central principle of Governance. (Its full flower as a conceptual tool is in the Tao.)

The internal combustion engine is a lower technology than steam where both are applicable, for it does less with more. As mathematicians say, it is less elegant. Lao-Tzu is quite specific about the virtues of the Way of Water. But we are greedy children with runaway power, and have no sense of taste. Still, at a sufficiently high level, technology's uses lead us sometimes towards one, willy-nilly.

Consider the handling of ephemeral information, on which our civilization is based. Currently we waste the planet's forests for our newspapers and a million periodicals. Video computers make possible a more sophisticated version of what the telephone network makes possible with messages: full information handling with only energy input, no materials to be wasted. True, the system's built and maintained with materials, though its operation is not: a burden shifted from the trees to the ore-bearing, oil-rich earth. But the raw-mineral base of electronics forms products which are eminently recyclable, and the technology sophisticates toward more art with less matter. When computer distribution stabilizes, a state only unbounded greed can avert, the industry can be made to depend on essentially a closed system of mineral use (given stable population) and on organic materials obtained from regenerative natural sources. These might include the managed forests which supply whatever computer printout cannot be expressed as microfilm or on recycled material. The housing industry is now the only other major predator of trees. Retechnologized construction would reduce its demands fivefold, whereupon they could also be satisfied by managed forests.

Taken together, these factors imply the total reconversion of the information industry, from resource wasting to resource sustaining. They also imply the possibility of reforesting literally half the continent (with the lesser part of this managed for lumber). And again the image beckons of a radically decentralized society living in a new integration with the natural ecology/order.

Our present technological capacities make possible such reconstruction of every human industry, to husband the earth's resources and operate in harmony with the delicate ecologies of life, amply and modestly. In the cases of housing and transportation, which together absorb a fifth of our industry, it is easiest to see that humanity's *present* industrial capacities, if re-engineered and redistributed, could provide for all mankind the adequacy of support they do for middle Americans. It is this vision—that we can eat our technological cake and have the world too, but have never really tried—which moves the players of Bucky Fuller's World Game. But like McLuhanism, Fullerism seems to take little account of the politics of power and our relation with the means of production, or of the deeper potentials for the freeing of our existence.

But the reharmonization of industry demands two things beyond the sharing of high technology: a psychology of recycling, and bounds to our desires—both products of our reconnection with the organic order of the world, and of reconciliation/balance with the Yin. So long as material industry is used for armor and to fill the void inside, our empowerment indeed condemns us to destroy.

Completeness compels a remark about energy. The usual question is whether we can continue to live on our gross and escalating energy budget. I agree, we can't, at least not the way we're getting it and spilling the waste. But if we tidy up, the amount we use is the false worry of hubris.

We think we're mighty, just because we can turn the sky black and threaten all earthlife. We are gnats in an infinitesimal film of mist on a great rock ball, spinning in space alive with energy. Each tiny shudder of earthskin releases more ergs than all our stockpiled weapons threaten. Until we come to tearing the very planet apart, our wildest uses of energy will be unnoticeable beside the sun.

Burning dead plants or leftover star matter is kid stuff. We begin to hook into the ongoing energy sources of the universe when we harness the tides for their power—a project which offers the easiest way of drawing energy in ecological harmony and which could begin for practical use with a year's military budget and effort.

CODA

Wandering between Lao-Tzu and the stars, it is difficult to grasp the immediacy of the future and the crisis of our choices about it.

Our industrial technologies are even now undergoing this transformation, but in a distorted Way. Already demand and manufacture are highly rationalized and integrated, and labor freed. But the greeds of power and profit outlaw Golem's development in ways which would mean his control by those whose production he reflects. Still, given present trends, in twenty years all but the poor of America *will be employing* an apparatus which makes mechanically possible a system of direct participation in political decision and radically decentralized education. The struggle between the freeing and the imprisoning uses of this apparatus will be tremendous, and crucial to our further development. It will determine the uses of the cyber-automation of our industry, which will take another twenty years, and the uses of the human energies radically freed by this transformation.

Twenty years, forty years. This century's examples of nations hell-bent on industrialization suggest that, if we chose, these conditions could be extended universally in forty or sixty years. At this point there would be no functional necessity for the human city—think that one over—and non-urban civilization would become possible.

The Tao is a technology of conception, a lens to reorganize vision. As such, it is a pragmatic tool for realizing social change, and one intention of these notes has been to soften the mystification which surrounds it. If Taoism references seem foreign to a discussion of technology and politics, that is because of the disrepute brought about by its false use as cover for the corruptions of the Chinese emperors, and because we in our categorical culture approach it as a "religion." True, the classic Taoist texts are usually read to warn against technological art. But they must be seen in their historical context, rather than as revealed Truth. They condensed at a time when the revolution to male dominance was still fresh in the culture, as an organizing node for the repressed Yin. For this reason the Taoist texts are not as balanced as their topic, and later commentators have seen them rightly as expounding a predominantly Yin social philosophy (in their dialectic with the culture's dominant Confucianism), a Way which puts least emphasis upon the Action in Inaction. There is also the matter of their having been formed in a time when conception and condition of technology were radically different. All in all, like Marx, Lao-Tzu needs to be brought up to date.

My references to Taoism do not constitute a serious attempt. Nor do I pretend to move well within the Way—nor to name it, whose superior workings are so simple, deep, and apparent as to be nearly invisible. But there is virtue in talking a bit about it, else Lao-Tzu would have held silent, and a few remarks on simple Taoist perspectives on social reconstruction may make the subterranean Taoism of these notes more visible.

—When the functional necessity of cities disappears, the organization of society in space is freed to seek new balance in the Tao of accumulation/dispersion. Social-psychological needs will lead to localized densities of habitation larger than the (extended) family group. But the largest such "towns" would be modest in size, for when the ratio of group population to the number of people a person can know grows too large or too small, group life becomes alienating. And such accumulations would pass more freely through the Tao of waxing and waning with time.

—In the Tao, it is not Nomad *versus* Urb, but a balancing of motion and rest, each generating the other. Both as a utopic cultural projection and in the most immediate and tangible personal senses, we are seeking a Way of life which cycles harmoniously between travel and indwelling, between City and Country, between community and isolation (and, beyond these to which material industry applies, is balanced in the polarities engagement/retreat, creation/reception, etc.).

—Though most achieve no new harmony, every new work group or living group now re-explores the Tao of private/shared, personal/group, as it structures architectural and social space. The first tendency generally is to overreact against the Yang, e.g., by leaving no one private space/time in a commune. But balance takes realistic account of our animal territorial needs.

—The matter of "property" is an exercise not only in the Tao of private/shared, but in the Tao of holding/letting go. Grasping it as personal armor against the Void, we are frozen in Yang attitude. But the children of the Bomb have come to new terms with the Void, and wear their hair Yin-soft and Yin-long. Raised vulnerable among radical abundance, they grow toward valuing objects for their beauty and use and being less reluctant to pass them on. An unpossessive psychology of property appeared in the Haight, and spreads.

—Considering any of our media of mass communications, we see that in their operation the Tao of affecting/being affected is frozen in imbalance, almost all Yang to the central controllers. It begins to be in balance in ham radio, or in talk-back radio with silent jockey and random call-selection.

—The concentration of energy is a natural process, and a necessary one for its dispersion: consider the initial investment of what we now describe as capital-and-labor, in the cybernated electronics plant. What is well distributed can be well put together, but for this balance to be maintained, must be well distributed again. This is scarcely the Way of Capitalism: energy accumulated generates with the object of more accumulation, rather than recirculation.

—As with communications, so with education, politics, etc.: present systems operate in fundamental imbalance in the Tao of leading/following, of affecting/receiving, and so on. It seems clear that when concentration of power/energy/information/-control becomes the permanent rather than transient condition of privileged nodes in a system—the condition I have referred to as "centralization" throughout—experience within it becomes isolated and fragmented, Divided. When the Tao of accumulation/dispersion operates freely among all nodes and through time, the system operates as a feedback network, and experience within it feels balanced in Division and Connection. Check it out.

—We build our houses to keep the outside out, not to blend inside/ outside in balance. Overall, our technology has arisen to divorce us from the rest of creation, rather than integrate us into all; to dominate rather than reciprocate or yield. Taoism affords a coherent perspective for resolving such contradictions of our uses.

Build something; indwell in it; express the experience. An exercise in the Tao of doing and resting, of creation and reception, of material and non-material work, of need and art. An experiment in the technology of writing, if you'll pardon my verbosity (the next stage is Diminishment). All I knew for starters was I had a paper due for a conference, and the kid needed a nursery first. I spent most of my weeks of building it just sitting around stoned among its pieces, its incomplete structure, staring at them dazedly, mind as blank as the Fool of the Hill. And then sat down under the butterfly, to have this come out, a bunch of struts and a thin skin, pieces of individual triangles which make a common chord of colors, not quite built like the standard house of an essay. Dear me, how Form does move within.

And other things as well, as I realize when I ask myself why so *many* words awkwardly striving for some coherent perspective should come out from me now, on this subject, in this time. And the phenomenon of media intervention in thought, most familiar to acidheads who listen to rock constantly, comes in the form of a story in the morning paper, this morning. It gives the first clear picture of upsurgent crisis in the technocratic ranks. Twenty years of radical overproduction have now run head-on into the cutback in aerospace programs, etc., caused by public reaction to the Military State. Elite unemployment is 10 percent and rapidly rising, bitterly discontented. Article predicts its energies will focus on the ecology movement and social reform, goes on to talk about how the cities are all messed up, need change. . . . On the front page of my family paper, no less.

Myself, when I left the technological priesthood I figured it would take at least a decade for me to seriously begin to try to recover for reuse the outer edge of the skills in which I'd been trained. I think every person who was raised inside the System and trained in specialized skills, and who has chosen to bolt role and move for freedom, faces this problem of how to reconvert his/her portion of the skills of the old Yang culture for liberating use; rather than just abandoning them (and a large part of the self) in flight, through seeing no way of using them without being involved in their whole original context. (But first must be slowly learned the skills we were denied, as foundation.) Half of my decade has passed now. In the presence of my newborn son and the dome, and at a time of trying to understand how to enter the future, through these notes my being comes together a first stage on this, and I begin the turnover for reentry, right on schedule. I wonder where and how I will accomplish it: playing in the cat-tail ecology of some pond we know with the other children, or mixing thermite and building electronic jamming devices in a ghetto underground bunker. At the moment, both images seem pretty strong.

PART THREE

Resources of the Religious Imagination

o

7

WHAT CAN THEOLOGY
CONTRIBUTE
TO AN ECOLOGICAL SOLUTION?

Brother David F. K. Steindl-Rast

On July 11, 1968 for the first time in history three Zen Roshis met in the West. Shunryu Suzuki Roshi, Hakuun Yasutani Roshi, and Soen Nakagawa Roshi came together at Tassajara Zen Mountain Center, all three agreeing that "the future of Zen lies in the West." It was the night of the midsummer full moon. Each one of the Roshis in turn was to address the students. What topic would each one choose on this historical occasion?

Soen Roshi began to speak: "I have just come from the bath house and I noticed the soap is left to soak in the soap dishes." And from this starting point he came to unfold his talk on waste and irreverence. One other remark from this historic speech stands out in my memory: "When we were novices, we would sweep the floor like you do. But my master said, 'This is not the way to do it. When you sweep you should do it as if you were saying to the dust, "pardon me, but you happen to be in the wrong place"—and then do it efficiently.' "

Reverence. That was the most outstanding characteristic of life at Tassajara the summer I spent there. A monk (a young American) with whom I was working in the garden was stung by a scorpion and made a deep bow to the little animal crawling away before he turned for help. This was the most dramatic example, but the reverence with which the young people there handled the garden tools, tied their sandals, or lifted the rice pots, though less dramatic, was even more impressive.

It was a surprise to see the young people (the same ones who used to slam car doors and litter the roadside with beer cans) live with such mindful reverence, but it was a greater surprise to find that in this central point the practice of Buddhist monks perfectly coincided with the very attitude towards which my whole training as a Benedictine monk had been geared.

The insight which emerged for me from these and similar experiences is simply that *East and West Meet in the Monastic Experience.* This insight led to a series of others which I would like to unfold here as I myself came to see it, step by step, in the course of my own development. I hope that this approach will not be subjective, but personal, and thereby more valid than mere objectivity.

What then do we mean by the monastic experience? The monastic experience is not foreign to any of us, but it is simply the expanding of a basic human dimension: the exploration of inner space. The seed for this quest lies in those moments of sudden awareness ("peak experience" is the current term) which all of us know. The monk devotes his whole life to the intense cultivation of this seed. Monastic life is a life-style centered in the peak experience. By analyzing the peak experience we would come to see that its liberating force springs from the removal of barriers, labels, separations. The core of this peak experience is the realization that *There Are No Gaps.* At the peak, one finds oneself one with oneself and one with all there is. There are no gaps.

The goal of all monastic training is integrity, and this integrity grows out of the realization that there are no gaps. To be struck by the fact that there are no gaps and to apply this insight radically to every area of daily life leads to what one might call the monastic life-style, and this is one way of living a truly human life. Some people (not very many) are psychologically predisposed to look for this radical life-style. They will become monks whether they live in a Buddhist, Christian, or Hindu environment. A given religion adds merely a particular emphasis to what is basically a human quest. To be a monk is simply one way of being human. At the point where the monk catches a glimpse of his goal, what lies at the very core of each religion reveals itself in a flash, because the goal in every case is ultimate Oneness.

Obviously, one does not have to become a monk in order to achieve integrity. However, unless any given culture strives in its own way for integrity which is the goal of monastic life it will not be able to avoid disaster. I have chosen this approach to our topic not only because it is the one congenial to me personally, as a monk, but also because the radical gaplessness of monastic life provides the opposite pole to that schizophrenic life-style which threatens to lead to Ecocatastrophe.

As for Christianity, the monastic angle is admittedly not the one from which it is most frequently viewed. However, what has come to be known as "monastic theology" is definitely in the ascendancy and is the only approach which promises to meet the demands of our situation. In the light of this theology, I come to see: *That There Are No Gaps Is the Gist of the Christian Message, for Christ Is the Ultimate Bond.* The Christian message centers not on what Christ teaches but on what he is: in Christian terms, Christ is the One who unites the cosmos to himself, and thus to God the Father. "For it was by God's own decision that the Son has in himself the full nature of God. Through the Son, then, God decided to bring the whole universe back to himself." (Col. 1:19–20, T.E.V.) "But when all things have been placed under Christ's rule, then he himself, the Son, will place himself under God, who placed all under him; and God will rule completely over all." (1 Cor. 15:28, T.E.V.)[1] It is hard to imagine a more succinct and clear statement of gapless unity than this unity seen by Christians as hinging on Christ.

But this approach leads to a startling discovery: the tension between the Christian message and the form in which it is presented. Theology by its very nature has a hard time getting beyond logical barriers, labels, and separations (which are often valid distinctions, carried one step too far), and yet it is in theological formulas that the Christian message most frequently reaches us. And the language of Christian theology happens to be that of Western philosophy; not as if Christian thought itself had not influenced and shaped wide areas of Western thought. Rarely, however, has it challenged and never fully overcome the inherent bias of what is basically a gap-philosophy.

One ought to show in this context that there exists an opposition between the body-soul dichotomy of Western thought and the body-soul unity in Judeo-Christian anthropology. Likewise the dichotomy of matter/spirit, sacred/profane, natural/super-natural, and similar polarizations is overcome by the very message of Christianity, while it remains indispensable for Western thought-structure. But, paradoxically, it is in this thought structure that the Christian message is being confined like the living egg within its lifeless shell. This means no less than that *The Christian Message Is Opposed to the Very Thought Structure Through Which It Is Transmitted.*

Gap-thinking, among its other effects, sets man over against his environment and so lies at the root of our ecological dilemma. Once I had come step by step to this point, it became evident that *No Judeo-Christian Belief, but Its Western Frame of Reference Constitutes an Ecological Hazard.*

I see a note of hope in the fact that within religion today the emphasis is shifting from Ethics to Spirituality. Somewhere in the past we must have started out by confusing religion and morality, man's search for meaningful life and the norms of meaningful living. From there on it was all too easy to allow religion to be swallowed up by ethics. In the end, organized religion at its worst no longer offered religious experience; it merely preached morality. Today people flock to where religious experience is made possible. They know once more what they want, and they will not settle for less. As I see it, then, *The Christian Experience Is Rapidly Getting Detached from an Exclusive Western Frame of Reference.*

This shift from Ethics to Religion does not imply a decline in morals. On the contrary, wherever it does take place it leads to a strengthening of moral fiber. Moral precepts are powerless unless they are anchored in the religious experience. Only a short time ago I witnessed several hundred young people listening in rapt attention to a Hindu Swami, who gave them a list of do's and don'ts which were anything but new. In fact, a nun who had apparently come with great expectations of esoteric wisdom was overheard whispering to her companion, "He is not saying anything our novice mistress has not said already." Why, then, would the young people accept it from the Swami? All sorts of superficial reasons might be adduced, but the only one that seems cogent to me is that for the ten preceding days the Swami had led them by a rather rigorous regime to that point (no matter how feebly glimpsed) from which ethics springs: the point of religious experience. R. M. Rilke, in his "Archaic Torso of Apollo," reveals the nexus between the enrapturing experience and the ethical imperative. All but the last two lines of the poem are a pure translation of the sculptured stone into word-music. The reader simply finds himself lost in a deep gaze at the sculpture which comes to life wherever the eye touches it. And now, suddenly, the stone becomes more than an object. Abruptly, but with perfect inner logic the poem is brought to a conclusion. "There is not one spot that does not look at you. You must change your life." This is not the great eye of justice under its frowning brow, but the eye of a lover, the glance of our true Self: deep, dreadful, sweet. And once we have encountered this glance, it is apt to meet us whenever our eyes truly touch reality, whenever we are truly ourselves, whenever we are truly present where we are. Every person, every thing, every situation— there is not one spot that does not look at you. Rules might change our outward behavior, but this awareness will change our life. *The Core of the Religious Experience Is Unlimited Mindfulness.* Limited mindfulness is the attitude by which we grasp things and situations. In unlimited mindfulness, we allow things and situations to take hold of us. The typical gestures corresponding to these two attitudes are the clenched fist grasping only so much and the open hand, ready to receive without limit. The basic religious gesture is the gesture of the open hand.

When this had become clear to me, I was ready to see a relationship between the great spiritual traditions which makes them dimensions of one another. In a miniature sketch, one could start again from the peak of experience. In it we suddenly became aware, "This is it!" And while THIS may be any person, any thing, any situation, IT is unlimited, stretching out toward ultimate meaning. Judaism, Christianity, Islam, whose spirituality focuses on the Word, will stress the THIS—the Word, the sign. Buddhism, saying the same, stresses the IT, the silent meaning. Hinduism, bridging the tension between the two by understanding, insists merely that this IS it.

From whatever angle we come to the awareness implied in the "This is It," wherever we place the emphasis, the result will be the same: mindfulness, awareness, reverence. And it is curious to see how a basic ethics springs directly from this awareness. Not to be aware, not to be truly present, can only have three causes, the three basic vices: hanging on to the past through greed, being ahead of oneself through impatience, or being indolent.

The connection between these vices and the present ecological crisis is all too obvious. Where resources are limited, greed prevents sharing. Rashness prevents planning. Indolence stifles caring and fosters idleness in the face of exploitation. If it is true that *Caring, Planning, and Sharing Spring from Mindfulness,* and that these three are the key to any ecological solution because ecology begins not with programs but with persons, it should be true also in the light of all that has been said here that *The Real Contribution of Religions to Ecology Lies Not in Preaching Ethics but in Leading to the Religious Experience.*

If this means that the contribution of theology is to overcome theology, that seeming loss will be our gain.

8
THE RETURN
OF THE
GODDESS

Everett E. Gendler

ARGUMENT IN BRIEF

In the West, one part of the problem of our relation to nature has to do with the suppression of the feminine. Note: "Feminine" and "female" or "woman" are not necessarily equivalent terms. "Feminine" is a quality which is found in females, but is found in males as well. We are all Yang and Yin, or, to cite a Western formulation: "When man is whole, both masculine and feminine are found in him" (Zohar I, 34b, my translation). The association of particular feminine traits and tasks with females is partly biological and partly sociocultural, but the ascription of feminine characteristics and functions exclusively to females is a culturally achieved distortion.

If Bachofen and Briffault are correct,[1] there was an early stage of mother-dominance, the domain of the feminine/female. This was succeeded by father-dominance, and the shift was psychic, symbolic, and social, for all are interrelated.

Psychically, the shift was away from matter, instinct, and the unconscious and toward spirit, rationality, and the conscious. Symbolically, the shift was away from night and moon and toward day and sun. Socially, the shift was away from property-in-common, inheritance through the mother, and agriculture and toward individual ownership, inheritance through the father, and city culture.

Crucial for our focus is the primordial association of the feminine with nature. Closely bound to soil and seedbed, the attack on the feminine (the goddesses) represented psychically an attack on the numinous quality of nature. The visible and the material were devaluated, and primarily the abstract and rational remained the locus of the sacred.

The Hebrew Bible comes on the scene at approximately the period of history when the struggle for masculine dominance has reached its peak. The Bible is here and there evidence of the struggle, but largely it is the justification of the shift to the new masculine-dominant order. This is part of the significance of the YHWH-only emphasis. A few feminine residues remain in Scripture, but evidences of earlier practices are found mostly in denunciations of the fertility religions, closely bound to soil and vegetation.

At the same time, it must be noted that the Hebrew Bible does not succumb to that flesh-spirit, body-mind split which has so devastated Western civilization.

". . . in Israelite thought man is conceived, not so much in dual fashion as 'body' and 'soul,' but synthetically as a unit of vital power or (in current terminology) a psycho-physical organism."[2]

The Bible represented a strong thrust toward consciousness, out of the uroboric state.[3] This was a necessary stage in human development psychically. However, long after the period when the battle was won, there has continued to be an influence which has been largely negative toward nature as numinous and toward the unconscious as valuable. This is hardly what we need today.

Our ecological plight, after all, is intimately related to our psychical plight, "the abstract conceptuality of modern consciousness . . . threatening the existence of Western mankind . . . The one-sidedness of masculine development has led to a hypertrophy of consciousness at the expense of the whole man."[4]

To re-dress the imbalance at this period of history requires psychic, symbolic, and social redress. Consequently, we find renewed interest in reclaiming some (not all) of the subterranean, suppressed feminine elements in Western religion. Rabbinic Judaism does, in fact, preserve a few of these, and Kabbalah and Hasidism strongly emphasize them. But we need the Bible as well.

For such purposes, then, it is helpful to read the Bible against the grain, as it were, and thereby reclaim, though obviously in a new context, those elements of the feminine which have persisted. In short, our motif at this stage of religion must be: no Spirit without Matter, and no gods/God without goddesses/the Goddess.

BACKGROUND IN BRIEF

YHWH is the tetragrammaton, the four-letter designation of the Divine in Hebrew Scripture. Consisting of four hardly audible Hebrew letters, its exact pronunciation was a secret once reserved to the High Priest, now lost. Yahweh and Jehovah are two common forms in English, the former preferred by scholars. There is, needless to say, an entire literature on the subject, but it is of distinctly secondary interest for this essay.

ADAMAH is the Hebrew word for "ground," and from it ADAM, "man," is clearly derived. In the Confessional, ADAMAH is personified. This is as much or as little a play on persons as is YHWH. In short, a literal interpretation of the Confessional is neither necessary nor precluded. The issue is not the form of theological expression (personal or nonpersonal), but rather its fairness (masculine balanced by feminine).

The attack on the feminine took place both astrally in the devaluation of the moon, and terrestrially in the devastation of the leafy groves. This is part of the meaning of the attack on idolatry. The centralization of worship prescribed in Deuteronomy is also an expression of this tendency, guarding against the reassertion of local cult practices, almost all of them rooted in the vegetation-fertility cycle.

The biblical allusions are numerous and must be left to the reader; hopefully most of them are evident. The few Rabbinic allusions are on the whole either self-explanatory or not essential to an understanding of the piece. One, perhaps, should be spelled out. The "double endowment with urges" refers to a Rabbinic doctrine concerning the ambivalent nature of man, and finds its scriptural support in the unusual spelling of "va-yii-tzer," "and He formed/impulsed" man (Gen. 2:7).

Linguistically, "d'char v'nukvah" is Aramaic for masculine and feminine. I use the Aramaic rather than the Hebrew ("zachar un'kevah") since *The Zohar,* the classic of Jewish mysticism which explores rather brilliantly aspects of the masculine-feminine balance, is written in Aramaic. Yang/Yin, of course, are the classic Taoist terms for the same polarity.

CONFESSIONAL

Then the LORD [YHWH] God [ELOHIM] formed a man [ha-a-dam] from the dust of the ground [ha-a-da-mah] . . .

(Gen. 2:7, N.E.B.)

. . . he came from the womb of mother earth . . .

(Eccles. 5:15, N.E.B.)

ADAMAH, Earth Mother, Mother of Adam, Mother of Man, Mother of birds, of beasts, of herbs and trees, we have wandered far away from you.

Drawn from You while formed by Him, bodied from You while imaged by Him, we—"d'char v'nukvah," masculine-feminine, Yang-Yin—should have been that "one flesh" by which YHWH and ADAMAH, Heaven and Earth, Sun and Moon, Spirit and Flesh, Consciousness and the Unconscious were forever joined. We, woman-man/man-woman, should have been that unbreakable link fused from the mating of YHWH and ADAMAH.

Vay-chu-lu ha-sha-ma-yim v'ha-a-retz . . .
And Heaven and Earth were wed . . .

(Gen. 2:1)[5]

Congelation of that conjoining, we, "d'char v'nukvah," were meant to maintain, in eternal renewal, that joyous and fruitful meeting.

But there was intrusion, and we erred; there was confusion, and we went astray. Where? How? Was it in eating from the fruit of the tree of distinctions? in redividing that which had been united? in splitting apart that which had been so joyously joined? in pitting Heaven versus Earth, Sun versus Moon, Spirit versus Flesh, Consciousness versus the Unconscious, Mind versus Instinct?

Why the urge to separate YHWH from connection with ADA-MAH? Why the insistence to deny His existence in Earth-form, visible, material, and tangible? Why such severe condemnation of El, of

Baal, of Tammuz, penultimate materializations of the Ultimately Im-
material?

Granted, there were abuses, mistakes, errors, even, let us admit,
human indignities. Quite true, some of the rites of fertility were far
from respectful of the full human being. Forgive us, Mother; pardon
us, Father. And yet . . .

Again we ask: Why the exile of YHWH in earthly form? Why
needed we prohibit His dallying with, His delighting in His beauteous
consort, ADAMAH? Was it jealousy on our part? a presumptuous,
prideful pretense to possess Her as exclusively ours? Why this strange
insistence that He abandon Her, abjure Her, write Her a bill of
divorcement?

> The heavens are the heavens of the Lord,
> While the earth He has given to the children of men.
>   (Ps. 115:16, my translation)

YHWH, all-too-indulgent Father, would that Your vaunted wrath had
intervened at this stage of the drama, forbidding us any further influence over You in this marital matter. But no, You humored us,
permitted us our distortions, to Your diminution and our own inde-
scribable hurt.

For what followed? Suspicion of the beautiful, now enforced by
the wrath born of Your bereavement, was loosed upon us. Oh so
quickly the banishment of Her in Her various vestments, each win-
some, each alluring, each enlivening. Asherah felled, Astarte
dimmed, the Queen of the Heavens blotted out. Like Father like Son:
dark bereavement.

> "A-ve-rah go-re-ret a-ve-rah." Misdeed begets misdeed.
>   (Abot 4:2, my translation)

YHWH dematerialized, He grows more remote. ADAMAH desacralized, She becomes common in our eyes, and soon contempt-
ible.

It begins in Heaven—or is it from Earth that it is cast upon
Heaven? No matter. Whichever the direction, the moon, "the purest
of earthly bodies and the impurest of heavenly bodies,"[6] the heavenly earth, as it were, is soon reduced in dignity. Invidious distinctions are introduced, rank doing indeed!

> . . . God made the two great lights, the greater to govern the day and
> the lesser to govern the night . . .
>
> (Gen. 1:16, N.E.B.)

What did such ranking mean for us?

> . . .the "diurnal domain of the mind" is dominated by solar symbolism
> . . . by a symbolism which . . . is often the result of a chain of reason-
> ing . . . The phases of the moon showed man time in the concrete
> sense . . .[7]

Of course, the abstract over the concrete!

> The sun is always the same, always itself, never in any sense "becom-
> ing." The moon, on the other hand, is a body which waxes, wanes and
> disappears, a body whose existence is subject to the universal law of
> becoming, of birth and death . . . "Becoming" is the lunar order of
> things.[8]

Of course, inflexible Being over fluid Becoming!

> . . . Man's integration into the cosmos can only take place if he
> can bring himself into harmony with the two astral rhythms, "unifying"
> the sun and moon in his living body . . . religious experience is not a
> priori incompatible with the intelligible. What is later and quite artificial
> is the exclusive primacy of reason.[9]

Such, then, the outcome of the ranking: discord now rending
what was formerly related in contrapuntal harmony.

But more was to follow. After depreciation came assault, denial,
destruction: War on the Queen of Heaven, the Moon.

> These are the words of the LORD of Hosts the God of Israel. . . . "Do
> not do this abominable thing which I hate." . . . Then all the men
> . . . and the crowds of women . . . answered Jeremiah: ". . . we will
> burn sacrifices to the queen of heaven and pour drink-offerings to her
> . . . making crescent-cakes marked with her image and pouring drink
> offerings to her." When Jeremiah received this answer . . . he said:
> "The LORD did not forget those sacrifices . . . they mounted up in his
> mind until he could no longer tolerate them. . . . Your land became a
> desolate waste, an object of horror and ridicule, with no inhabi-
> tants. . . ."
>
> (Jer. 44: 2,5,15–16, 19–23, N.E.B.)

Father, were you really so wroth? Did we hear You truly? Did we not
tragically misunderstand?

Nowhere in the history of religions do we find an adoration of any natural object in itself. A sacred thing, whatever its form and substance, is sacred because it reveals or shares in ultimate *reality*. Every religious object is always an "incarnation" of something: of the *sacred.*[10]

Father, She being denied You, we also lost Her. You, perhaps, survived, depleted but not devastated. But we began to find ourselves cut off from that of our selves which abided in Her.

It might be said that the moon shows man his true human condition; that in a sense man looks at himself, and finds himself anew in the life of the moon.[11]

Wrath loosed in Heaven soon afflicted Earth, for are They not, in we, One? "Adam encompasses above and below" (Zohar I, 34b, my translation). War on vegetation when it revealed too verdantly Your great, rhythmic renewals!

You shall demolish all the sanctuaries where the nations whose place you are taking worship their gods, on mountain-tops and hills and under every spreading tree. You shall pull down their altars and break their sacred pillars, burn their sacred poles and hack down the idols of their gods and thus blot out the name of them from that place.

(Deut. 12:2–3, N.E.B.)

Mother, how we treated You!

All this was accompanied by cult centralization, the insistence that the great gifts of spirit, dematerialized, were the better to be found in Temple confines than on verdant heights.

. . . you shall resort to the place which the LORD your God will choose out of all your tribes to receive his Name that it may dwell there. There you shall come and bring your whole-offerings and sacrifices . . . There you shall eat before the LORD your God . . . you shall bring everything that I command you to the place which the LORD your God will choose as a dwelling for his Name . . . See that you do not offer your whole-offerings in any place at random, but offer them only at the place which the LORD will choose in one of your tribes . . .

(Deut. 12:4–6, 7, 11, 13 N.E.B.)

No more the companionship of You, Mother, and Him, with sanctity widespread; no more those precious material gifts of spirit bestowed by You and Him together: the recurrent *miracle* of growth renewed.

And suspicion, consuming suspicion of the beauteous, culminating in Rabbi Akiba's dictum:

> Wherever you find a lofty mountain, a high hill,
> or a spreading tree, there you will find idolatry.
>
> (Abodah Zarah 3:5, my translation)

Desacralized and devaluated, how we treated Her! Mother, cast off not in old age but while yet young and beautiful! Did we "cultivate and care for" You? (Gen. 2:15) Those were the words of our Father, were they not? But we chose instead to practice "dominate" and "subdue" (Gen. 1:26–28). Father, which was truly You speaking? Mother, how we betrayed You both!

Did we share Your bounty with our brothers, the beasts? The charnel stench of this planet's slaughter is answer enough. Birds, beasts, and fish; alien tribes, fellow men, and brothers: who has escaped our minded murders? How quickly the earth was corrupted and filled with violence (Gen. 6:13). And how soon we rewrote Scripture to legitimate the slaughter (Gen. 9:2–3).

That, of course, is not the whole story. How could it be? Were we not doubly endowed with urges? There was, all along, a continuing impulse to consider You.

> When you enter the land which I give you, the land shall keep sabbaths to the LORD. For six years you may sow your fields and for six years prune your vineyards and gather the harvest, but in the seventh year the land shall keep a sabbath of sacred rest, a sabbath to the LORD.
>
> (Lev. 25:2–4, N.E.B.)

That ADAMAH and YHWH share together the joys of the Sabbath!

The moon, too, Your luminous counterpart, was ever respected by the folk. Monthly Her renewal was celebrated out of doors as the people exulted in the light of Her Presence. Even the Rabbinic tradition conceded the point.

> In the school of Rabbi Ishmael it was taught: Had Israel merited no other privilege than greeting the Presence of their heavenly Father once a month (by reciting the benediction over the renewed moon), they would be contented!
>
> (Sanhedrin 42a, my translation)

There are many other elements as well, ADAMAH, which seek Your preservation and reflect concern for You. Yet basically, Mother,

ADAMAH, in trying to steal You from YHWH, to seize and possess You, to lay exclusive, incestuous claim to You, all we managed was to dispossess ourselves. For You were not destined to be possessed absolutely by man. "The land is mine" says YHWH (Lev. 25:23, N.E.B.).

How presumptuous we were: reducing YHWH to entire rather than to Ultimate Invisibility! denying the enlivening intermediate forms! With what results? YHWH reduced to ever-unseen deity, the *tzelem* (image of God) not taken seriously, and You, ADAMAH, dissected into chemical components: N, K, P!! Sentience, sensibility, and joy removed, cosmic harmonies drowned out by the roar of earthly machines, and our own connections with You severed.

Once upon a time, ADAMAH, we sensed the life coursing through You and related to You respectfully, lovingly, though not idolatrously.

> . . . earth itself is alive . . . The relation between the earth and its owner is not that the earth, like a dead mass, makes part of his psychic whole —an impossible thought. It is a covenant-relation, a psychic community, and the owner does not solely prevail in the relation. The earth has its nature, which makes itself felt, and demands respect. The important thing is to deal with it accordingly and not to ill-treat it . . . The task of the peasant is to deal kindly with the earth, to uphold its blessing, and then take what it yields on its own accord. If he exhausts it, then he attacks its soul and kills it; after that it will only bring forth thorns, thistles and whatever else pertains to the wilderness.[12]

Once upon a time, ADAMAH, we sensed the true ideal as well: every man under his own vine and fig tree:

> . . . they shall beat their swords into plowshares,
> and their spears into pruning-hooks;
> nation shall not lift up sword against nation,
> neither shall they learn war any more.
> . . . and each man shall dwell under his own vine,
> under his own fig tree, undisturbed.
> For the LORD of Hosts himself has spoken.
> (Mic. 4:3–4, partially taken from A.S.V. and N.E.B.)

Idyllic and right, ideal and peaceful. How much might have been accomplished had we but maintained that intimacy with You, ADAMAH. The preparation of the soil, the planting of the seed, the protection of the tender shoot: caring and nurturing Your activities,

Your image, our Yin, there for our acceptance. Defoliation might have come harder to us, mightn't it? The motherly in each of us might have been preserved.

> At the lowest, darkest stages of human existence the love between the mother and her offspring is the bright spot in life, the only light in the moral darkness, the only joy amid profound misery . . . The relationship which stands at the origin of all culture, of every virtue, of every nobler aspect of existence, is that between mother and child; it operates in a world of violence as the divine principle of love, of union, of peace. Raising her young, the woman learns earlier than the man to extend her loving care beyond the limits of the ego to another creature, and to direct whatever gift of invention she possesses to the preservation and improvement of this other's existence.[13]

Each man under his own vine and fig tree. And even the legislation to insure it, given by YHWH Himself, sentiment alone not being sufficient.

> You shall count seven sabbaths of years, that is seven times seven years, forty-nine years . . . and you shall send the ram's horn round. You shall send it through all your land to sound a blast, and so you shall hallow the fiftieth year and proclaim liberation in the land for all its inhabitants. You shall make this your year of jubilee. Every man of you shall return to his patrimony, every man to his family . . . When you sell or buy land amongst yourselves, neither party shall drive a hard bargain . . . No land shall be sold outright, because the land is mine, and you are coming into it as aliens and settlers. Throughout the whole land of your patrimony, you shall allow land which has been sold to be redeemed.
>
> (Lev. 25:8–11, 14–15, 23–24, N.E.B.)

So there it stands, ADAMAH, linked directly with Your Sabbaths! How much that might have done both for You and for us: fewer large landholdings, fewer dispossessed peasants, fewer exploited poor, fewer cruel accumulations of wealth; and fewer inhuman concentrations of humans cut off from You, fewer people removed from the magic of Your great cycle of birth-growth-ripeness-death-rebirth, fewer people totally passive and dependent on others in the getting of their basic nourishment, fewer human beings totally surrounded by mechanisms rather than growing-fruiting-living beings.

Factory farming? Why? Monoculture? For what reason? Pesticides, lethal to insects and us alike? No need. Your preferred small holdings would have obviated these damaging developments. Pollution of our air by transports bringing our sorry foodstuffs from chemicaled countryside to choking cities? Unimaginable! Mother, to what orphaned state are we reduced!

Rabbi Ahai ben Josiah says:

> He who purchases grain in the market place,
> to what may he be likened?
> To an infant whose mother dies:
> although he is taken from door to door to other
> wet nurses, he is not satisfied . . .
> He who eats of his own is like an infant
> raised at its mother's breast.
>
> (Abot de Rabbi Nathan, Ch. 30)[14]

But finally, to what end this weeping? For could it have been otherwise? Without some such break away from You, dark, encompassing Earth Mother, without some such thrust, would the Heaven in us have been felt at all? Might we not have spent our lives, generation after generation, in benighted bondage to You, anxious, fearful, unaware, infantile dependents? There is, after all, Your fearsome face as well as Your gracious one, Your devouring nature as well as Your sustaining one: drought and disease were not unknown to us. These, You realize, we had to contend with, that we might become Your mature collaborators rather than abject dependents. You are great, ADAMAH, but perhaps You, too, like Him, prefer us as partners, not subjects. And so we imagined, fantasied, rationalized, and reasoned our way to some measure of control over You, ADAMAH. Had we any choice?

Yet it is painfully clear now: the measure is too full, the break too complete, and we have strayed so far away from You that we now fear for our own lives, not to speak of Yours. As with our Zulu brothers, our being "far away" means: "There where someone cries out, 'O mother, I am lost.' "[15]

> O ADAMAH, Earth Mother,
> Mother of Adam, Mother of all men,
> Mother of birds, of beasts, of trees,
> we have wandered far away from You.
>
> O Great One, from Whose womb we at first emerged,
> O Mother of all living, whence we too came:
> if we pare away pretense, pride, and presumption,

if we end exploitation and embrace appreciation,
if we weed out coercion and cultivate gentleness:
May we once again, yet as never before,
return to You, and with You to Him?
May we once again, yet as never before,
unite in ourselves
Spirit and Flesh,
Conscious and Unconscious,
Sun and Moon,
Heaven and Earth,
d'char v'nukvah,
yang and yin,
male and female?

If so, then again, yet as never before,
You and He shall unite once more;
and once again, yet as never before,
the morning stars will sing together
while all Your children shout for joy.

DISCUSSION IN BRIEF

Had we in the West managed somehow to take at full value "Av ha-ra-cha-mim," one classical Rabbinic form of address to the Divine (or its equivalent), the foregoing remythicization might have been unthinkable. "Av ha-ra-cha-mim" is usually translated "Merciful Father," but etymologically the more literal and more revealing translation is "Wombed Father." The phrase implies, in other words, a unification of the masculine and feminine elements in the Single Person. The value of this kind of monotheism for the full human being can hardly be overestimated, and it is toward this that we must work, it seems to me, both theologically and personally. However, in view of the fact that Western religion has tended to achieve "unification" of the masculine and feminine elements largely by simple masculine domination of the feminine, there may be some warrant for the foregoing Confessional. At the very least, it makes the individual elements of "d'char v'nukvah" available once again for a more satisfactory integration.

The direct ecological implications of this should not be underestimated:

In a patriarchate . . . matter is regarded as something of small value in contrast to the ideal—which is assigned to the male-paternal side.

. . . Unnatural symbols and hostility to the nature symbol . . . are characteristic of the patriarchal spirit. . . . The matriarchal spirit does not deny the native maternal soil from which it stems. It does not, like the Apollonian-solar-patriarchal spirit, present itself as "sheer being," as pure existence in absolute eternity, but . . . apprehending itself as historically generated, as a creature, it does not negate its bond with the Earth Mother.[16]

To re-claim the matriarchal spirit and our bond with the Earth Mother strikes me as necessary if we are to address at all successfully the ecological crisis confronting us. As we are now, split within, our world too is split. Distrustful of our bodies, Earth's body frightens us. Devaluing matter (however obscenely we accumulate), we maltreat our planet. Cut off from layers of our selves, the world as well seems alien.

To heal the breach will require both religious reconsideration and a social policy concerning numbers and distribution of population which will permit all of us some significant relation to the soil.

One final note of clarification. None of the reopening of this religious question in any way denies the great advance which Hebrew prophecy brought to men. While dematerialization may have been in the theological sphere carried rather too far, the widespread tendency of ancient paganism to identify the king with the god was generally warrant for social oppression of a thoroughly distasteful kind, including the unconscionable accumulation of land. Furthermore, there was a tendency to determinism in ancient nature cults which also had to be confronted.

We must never forget that the emphasis on distributive justice and secure small holdings, so central to the biblical outlook as expressed in the Sabbatical and Jubilee legislation, in this respect relates the prophetic tradition most positively to both the ecological and the social issues of our own age.

9

TOWARD A POETICS OF ECOLOGY: A SCIENCE IN SEARCH OF RADICAL METAPHORS

Richard A. Underwood

SOME REMINISCENCES

When I was in high school in a little town of some two thousand persons in northeastern Indiana, I had a morning paper route. On one section of the route on the north side of town, all of the houses faced the east, overlooking a meadow which was part of one of the largest farms in the area. One spring morning I was devoting complete attention, during this section of the route, to finishing as quickly as possible. Suddenly the springtime called out. A meadowlark's song broke the silence of the time and place and penetrated my consciousness. I turned and saw him perched on the fence which bordered the meadow. At the moment of my turning, the morning sun was just fully risen and the meadowlark was perfectly centered against the background of the sun—as if the bird itself were the present of the sun and its song the voice of the sun. The scene disappeared instantly as I rode on; but the song and the vision lingered. As I threw a paper onto the porch of the next house I thought to myself: here is a message from the sun, through the bird, through me, to you—only you won't know it.

The sense of this episode was soon, unfortunately, forgotten. I did not have occasion to remember it until many years later, some fifteen to eighteen years later, as a matter of fact, during the later stages of graduate school. In the course of my reading, I came across two passages which reawakened me to some of the meanings of the episode just recounted—one passage from a psychologist, the other from a poet.

The psychologist was C. G. Jung, writing of an experience he had had in the region of East Africa:

> . . . I believe that, after thousands and millions of years, someone had to realize that this wonderful world of mountains and oceans, suns and moons, galaxies and nebulae, plants and animals, *exists*. From a low hill in the Athi plains of East Africa I once watched the vast herds of wild animals grazing in soundless stillness, as they had done from time immemorial, touched only by the breath of a primeval world. I felt then as if I were the first man, the first creature, to know that all this *is*. The entire world round me was still in its primeval state; it did not know that it *was*. And then, in that one moment in which I came to know, the world sprang into being; without that moment it would never have been. All Nature seeks this goal and finds it fulfilled in man, but only in the most highly developed and most fully conscious man. Every advance, even the smallest, along this path of conscious realization adds that much to the world.[1]

Reading this passage reminded me of my experience on that spring morning. I saw that what I had earlier experienced—but had neither the sensitivity nor the vocabulary to articulate—was an expansion of and deepening of awareness, the awareness of a sense of participation in "the great chain of being." I saw also, at least I *thought* I saw, that the preoccupation with my own individuality and the tasks I had set for myself, both for that spring day and for the years which followed, cut me off from, isolated me from the sense of participation in a cosmic order which stretched from the sun, through the bird, through me, and to the person for whom I was leaving the morning paper.

Some two years after reading this passage from Jung I was introduced to the poetry of Wallace Stevens. With no expectation whatsoever that also it would reawaken the long ago experience of that spring morning, I found myself reading one of Stevens' last poems, "Not Ideas About the Thing But the Thing Itself":

At the earliest ending of winter,
In March, a scrawny cry from outside
Seemed like a sound in his mind.

He knew that he heard it,
A bird's cry, at daylight or before,
In the early March wind.

. . . .

That scrawny cry—it was
A chorister whose c preceded the choir.
It was part of the colossal sun,

Surrounded by its choral rings,
Still far away. It was like
A new knowledge of reality.*

A high school boy, a paper route, a spring morning, a meadow-lark, a rising sun, a psychologist's reminiscence of East Africa, a poet's construction, or reconstruction, of a morning at "the earliest ending of winter." It is all idiosyncratic. But the deepest dimension of idiosyncrasy is surrounded by the unity of the All, that which is "part of the colossal sun." Imbedded somewhere in all of this are radical metaphors which inform a poetics of ecology. What follows is an attempt to bring them to view.

ECOLOGICAL CRISIS AND METAPHORS GONE AWRY

Part of the scene of the ecological crisis involves the reception of messages from the sun and the stars, the moon, the sea, the air, and the earth. The messages pass through the medium of man's presence—articulated by his metaphors—and the impact of the message is one of distortion, imbalance, pollution. It is as if Jesus' observation had been vindicated on a colossal scale in our own time:

> O generation of vipers, how can ye, being evil, speak good things? for out of the abundance of the heart the mouth speaketh. A good man out of the good treasure of the heart bringeth forth good things: and an evil man out of the evil treasure bringeth forth evil things.
>
> (Matt. 12:34–35, K.J.V.)

It is clear, I trust, that what has been brought forth out of the heart of technological man is *evil*. It is evil in the *moral* sense: think of the American continent—the deracination of Indian, buffalo, peregrine falcon, sea osprey. This is no mere romanticization of nature's original, prehuman state. It is rather a question: is *this* why man appeared on the scene—to be able to say that what *is* is life destructive? It is also evil in the *ontological sense*. What has been done is sorrowful enough. But what has been done may still be redeemed. What is *more* sorrowful is what this state of affairs shows as man's state or mode of being: *his forgetfulness of being* (to borrow a phrase from that preeminently ecological theorist, Martin Heidegger), his concentration upon rational control, to the exclusion of the power of irrationality, his assumption (under a false assumption of ego strength which might be interpreted as an evolutionary aberration) that his subjective intention, based on only 6,000 years of conscious historical experience, is more trustworthy than the aeons of evolution which preceded man's appearance and made this appearance *possible*. Since it made possible man's appearance with his typically self-aggrandizing claim to exclusively intelligent consciousness, is evolution then to be deemed *un*intelligent?

This raises the question of *how* the man of advanced industrial civilization at the present stage of North American democracy organizes his life. Does he do so with a sense of himself as the extension of, a participant in, the energy which moves the sun, stars, moon, tides, earth, blood, and breath? Or does he do so under the aegis of metaphors that make him *feel* himself as antagonist to these same energies? A response—if not an answer—to this question is to be found in a column by James Reston in the August 30, 1970, edition of The New York *Times*. Mr. Reston is reflecting on some of the problems raised during the August 1970 session of the Aspen Institute for Humanistic Studies in Colorado. Mr. Reston indicates that the Institute engaged in examining and questioning, among other things, the following widely held beliefs:

1. Air and water are free commodities.
2. Most land and the resources on it and under it may be used in accordance with the unrestricted desires of its private owners.

3. Economic development should proceed along lines largely determined by private initiative.
4. Economic decisions in America should be left primarily to the interplay of market forces.
5. And finally: continuous economic growth will inevitably produce a continuous growth in social well-being; and a growing population will both stimulate and benefit from economic expansion.

What kind of world do these "widely held beliefs" indicate? It is a world which reflects at least the following:
1. Whatever is in the world is free for the taking.
2. Private and subjective wishes, defined as individual initiative, take precedence over any claim of collective integrity—whether it be in the realm of *society* or the realm of *nature*.
3. Growth, development, and increase depend not so much on modes of cooperation, a fundamental sense of union and participation in a transcendent unity, as upon *conflict* and *competition*. Further, the *resolution* of the antagonism implicit in both is achieved by superior shrewdness and overwhelming power of one sort or another. It is summed up in the adage: nothing succeeds like success (and success is all that matters).

Two or three observations are in order as to how the metaphors implicit in these "widely held beliefs" relate directly to the ecological crisis.

A. Are not the metaphors implicit in the "widely held beliefs" ultimately responsible for the environmental crisis which we now face? That is, has not a premium been placed upon the values of competition, individual rights, aggressiveness, manipulation, and eventually *control*? Do not *all* of these terms involve violence and exploitation to some degree? Are not these precisely the modes which technology depends upon for its "cultural justification"?

B. Are not the metaphors implicit in the "widely held beliefs" contrary to the *theoretical virtues* of the tradition which produced the era of scientific technology? Namely: the tradition of Western civilization, founded in the Greco-Roman Judeo-Christian values which emphasized love, compassion, understanding, toleration, cooperation, and justice?

C. If the metaphors implicit in the "widely held beliefs" (did they *issue in* or *follow from* the ethos of technology) *are* contrary to the theoretical virtues of the classical dimensions of the foundation of Western culture, *then* does it not follow that the environmental crisis currently experienced is one *not* of technology but a metaphor? That is, is not the environmental crisis to be resolved by a change of attitude and metaphor which would then inform the nature and dynamics of technological planning, enabling it to be an extension of, a reenforcement of (not a contradiction of), the theoretical virtues of the founding traditions of Western culture? In *this* mode, technology might then become a tender of, a carer for, a lover of, an understander of the nature we seek to transform into a reality more harmonious with the wishes of a supposedly enlightened human intelligence.

FAUST AND DESCARTES:
METAPHORICAL ORIGINS OF THE ECOLOGICAL CRISIS

To speak of the ecological crisis as a crisis of *metaphor,* and only secondarily as a crisis of *technology,* reveals a different dimension of the crisis. It also provides a direction as to where we are to look for some clue as to the origins of "the widely held beliefs" that constitute the ethos of technological analysis and application. It would be not so much the history of science; instead, the tack being followed here is that the emergence of scientific technology is itself based upon a prior commitment to a new metaphor, the full implications of which become visible only in the shape of the developing technology. Thomas S. Kuhn, in his book *The Structure of Scientific Revolutions,* makes somewhat the same point, but with different intentions. He speaks not of metaphor but of *paradigm* and *paradigm shift.* He observes that, led by a new paradigm, scientists adopt new instruments and look in new places. Even more important, during the revolutions scientists see new and different things when looking with familiar instruments in places they have looked before.[2]

As distinct from Mr. Kuhn's attempt, the questions *we* are asking here are: where do the *metaphors* come from, how do they affect new scientific techniques, and how do they become diffused throughout a culture as "widely held beliefs" (a world view) which in turn reenforce the ethos of scientific technology?

Besides standing in need of further refinement, these questions are much too ambitious to be pursued here. I will not, then, attempt to answer them. I will, however, appeal to two figures, Faust and Descartes, as a brief and tentative illustration of procedures of interpretation I see involved in our questions.

The case of Faust is particularly relevant to the question of *metaphor formation* and *ecological crisis*. Goethe's *Tragedy of Faust* begins with Faust at his desk, observing that he has studied philosophy, jurisprudence, medicine "and even, alas! Theology." But he observes also that he knows no more now than he did before —the issue being the nature of his knowing. He says:

> These ten years long, with many woes,
> I've led my scholars by the nose,—
> And see that nothing can be known!
> *That* knowledge cuts me to the bone.[3]

Faust then announces he will appeal to magic . . .

> That I may detect the inmost force
> which binds the world, and guides its course;
> Its germs, productive powers explore,
> And rummage in empty words no more.

In retrospect, we can see that the magic (involving also, of course, Faust's compact with Mephistopheles) becomes the instrument (the magic wand) by which the modern world seeks to "detect the inmost force which binds the world, and guides its course." This intention, of course, is not new: it marks the history of thought from the earliest Egyptian and Babylonian and Greek myth-makers, astrologists, geometers, philosophers, and theologians. *However,* this opening scene of Faust traces the shift from the medieval to the modern world—a shift from the metaphor of *knowing* to the metaphor of *making* or *doing,* a shift from *Homo sapiens* to *Homo faber.* That is, what Faust is seeking is a more satisfying understanding of knowledge, knowledge as power of action, not simply as power of abstract thought. This is illustrated in Faust's toying with the possibility of a new translation of the prologue to the Gospel of St. John— which is ironic in view of the fact that earlier he had vowed no more

to "rummage in empty words." Apparently he intuited that the Word of the Book he was reading was not merely "empty words." Faust tries two alternatives to the original "In the Beginning was the *Word*";
1) a first alternative: "In the Beginning was the Thought."
2) a second alternative: "In the Beginning was the Power."
Then he observes:

> Yet, as I write, a warning is suggested,
> That I the sense may not have fairly tested.
> The Spirit aids me: now I see the light!
> 'In the Beginning was the *Act*,' I write.

The second person to be adduced as instructive in the question of metaphor-formation as it relates to the ecological crisis is Descartes. We have been appealing to Goethe's *Faust*. The "real" Faust antedated Descartes by roughly a century. I am speaking in terms of images, not strict historical cause and effect relationship, a transition during what we could call now a common *Zeitgeist*, when I say that Descartes is the Faust-image brought to *real life*. This is most strikingly illustrated in a passage in part VI of Descartes' *Discourse on Method*. Part VI of the *Discourse* is organized around questions which will advance further the investigations of nature (a counterpoint to Faust's desire to "detect the inmost force which binds the world and guides its course"). There is, as a matter of fact, a close correlation between the *sentiment* expressed by Faust in Goethe's scene 1 and that expressed by Descartes in the following passage:

> . . . it is possible to attain knowledge which is very useful in life and . . . instead of that speculative philosophy which is taught in the Schools, we may find a practical philosophy by means of which, knowing the force and action of fire, water, air, the stars, heavens and all other bodies that environ us . . . we can . . . *render ourselves the masters and possessors of nature.*[4]

This passage from Descartes, I submit, is the *locus classicicus* for understanding the metaphors which inform both the nature of scientific technology and the "widely held beliefs." Left to itself, the history of science could have been a continuation of classical Greek and scholastic intentions: the desire of an intellectual elite simply to *understand*. Galileo, for instance, recanted publicly his conclusion, based upon empirical observation, that the earth moves. Under his breath, however, he is reported to have said, "But it moves." This seems to indicate a view toward scientific exploration and analysis under the *old* mode: knowledge for knowledge's sake, and the public(ation) be damned. Under the imaginations of Faust and Descartes, however, the private intention becomes public and aggressive: to transform speculative knowledge into the power of possession, mastery, and control!

What I am suggesting is this: it is not the act of Galileo's telescope, but, rather, the metaphors of the Faustian and Cartesian imagination that are ultimately responsible for the ecological crisis currently being experienced. The ecological crisis, that is, issues from the "fact" that we remain hypnotized by Faust and Descartes. The implication, of course, is this: we must wake up and seek *new* metaphors. Only as we free ourselves from the power of the Faustian and Cartesian imagination will we be able to resolve the ecological crisis. That is: *both* the Faustian *and* the Cartesian imagination place a premium upon knowledge as act and mastery and possession of nature *to the exclusion of any sense of self-understanding* which sees self as participating intimately in that "inmost force" which both imaginations seek to understand and control. The desire of the Faustian and Cartesian imagination to control nature is based upon an understanding of man as a being alienated from nature. This is the first and radical step toward what we now experience as the ecological crisis. The effects of this first step were not particularly noticeable at the early stages. It was not until the massive technological intervention of the middle third of the twentieth century, into the processes of ecological balance, that the effects of the Faustian and Cartesian metaphors became undeniably present. These effects include overpopulation, urban decay, pollution of water, air, and earth. As an incidental observation: probably at no time since the pre-Socratic cosmologists some twenty-five centuries ago has Western man become so aware of the precarious balance of the original elements of fire, air, earth, and water. The difference, however, is crucial: the pre-Socratic awareness proceeded from a sense of wonder at what IS. The awareness emerging in the midst of the ecological crisis, in typical twentieth-century dialectical fashion, proceeds from wonder at what is *absent* or *lacking*. It is interesting to consider whether we could wonder about what is absent if the pre-Socratics had not wondered about what IS!

POETICS AND ECOLOGY:
TOWARD THE RECOVERY OF LIFE-GIVING METAPHORS

I would like to return now, to the introductory reminninscences.

During the course of writing this essay, two events have intruded themselves. The first is a twenty-minute bicycle ride with my nine-year-old daughter. We could have cycled to Hartford's Elizabeth Park, with its rose gardens, duck pond, and flowers. But we had contracted to get milk for breakfast. So we rode to and along the Avenue. We participated, in our bicycle ride, in the dynamics—with all of its noises, foul smells, litter, and local dangers, namely traffic—of our immediate environment. While we were riding, and having a very nice time, I remembered this paper I was supposedly in the midst of writing. And I was sad, at first, that I could not, as I had been able to do nearly thirty years ago in my high school town, ride for three minutes and find a rising sun, a meadow, and a meadowlark. But then I remembered: even in the midst of those gifts I had been preoccupied with my own routine, with pursuing my own subjective intentions. When the song of the meadowlark broke the morning stillness I paid attention only momentarily. It took—in the course of the next fifteen years—a psychologist and a poet to remind me of the revelation. So—to return to the bicylce ride with my daughter along the main east-west avenue of Hartford—I decided: this is her environment. It needs changing and cleaning. I want her to see the sun rising and setting, to feel the pull of the tides, to see the stars, and to know the momentary joy of a bird's song. Now, however, this may be the vocation of the poet: to recall all of this to her. But even more importantly: she must discover that even the sound of an automobile exhaust participates in the same energies I experienced, in a completely different setting, some thirty years ago.

The second event—after returning from the ride, helping to put the children to bed, and thinking again about this paper—was watching the television program *Bonanza*. I say it unabashedly: I *like* Ben Cartwright, the Ponderosa, and the events portrayed of late nineteenth-century Colorado frontier becoming civilization. As I watched

and remembered the paper to which I knew I must return, I thought
in the final analysis the function of this program *(Bonanza)* is to keep
alive the memory of an earlier order, without being hypnotized by
it. And then—upon returning to my desk—I turned to this passage
in Goethe's *Faust:*

> Two souls, alas! reside within my breast,
> And each withdraws from, and repels, its brother.
> One with tenacious organs holds in love
> And clinging lust the world in its embraces;
> The other strongly sweeps, this dust above,
> Into the high ancestral spaces. (Scene ii)

In the course of this essay, I have tried to show that the ecological crisis is one primarily and fundamentally of metaphor. By *both*
implication *and* direct statement, I have also intimated that the *resolution* of the ecological crisis is to be found in a recovery and/or
restoration of metaphor. Science does not invent metaphors, it formulates technique. Science—without which we cannot live—*lives
out* metaphor. The resolution of the ecological crisis depends, then,
upon the extent to which life-giving metaphors can be restored to our
communal life. It seems fitting, then, to end with these lines by a poet
who, though he speaks of the kingdom of poetry, might well be
speaking of the sovereignty of metaphor:

> For poetry is like light, and it is light.
> It shines over all, like the blue sky, with the same blue justice.
> For poetry is the sunlight of consciousness:
> It is also the soil of the fruits of knowledge
>   In the orchards of being:
> It shows us the pleasures of the city.
> It lights up the structures of reality.
> It is a cause of knowledge and laughter:
> It sharpens the whistles of the witty:
> It is like morning and the flutes of morning, chanting and enchanted.
> It is the birth and rebirth of the first morning forever.*

*From *Summer Knowledge,* New and Selected Poems 1938–1958 by Delmore
Schwartz. Copyright © 1968 by Delmore Schwartz. Reprinted by permission of
Doubleday & Company, Inc.

NOTES

CHAPTER 1

1. Aldo Leopold, "Lakes in Relation to Terrestrial Life Patterns," *Symposium on Hydro-Biology* (Madison: University of Wisconsin Press, 1941).

2. R. S. Miller, "How Many People," *Bulletin No. 76,* Yale University School of Forestry, 1970, pp. 5–17.

3. Aldo Leopold, *Game Management* (New York: Charles Scribner's and Sons, 1933).

4. William R. Burch, "Some Sociological Observations on the Environmental Crisis," *Bulletin No. 76,* Yale University School of Forestry, 1970, pp. 30–54.

5. Miller, *op. cit.*

6. Lester Brown, unpublished, undated manuscript.

7. G. W. Thomas, "The Ecology of Food Production—Can the World Afford to Feed Itself?" *ICASALS Contribution No. 79,* International Center for Arid and Semi-Arid Land Studies, Lubbock, Texas, 1970.

8. *Ibid.*

9. T. W. Box and G. W. Thomas, *Social and Ecological Implications of Water Importation in Arid Lands in Perspective* (Tucson: University of Arizona Press, 1969).

10. R. H. Whittaker, *Communities and Ecosystems* (New York: The Macmillan Co., 1970), p. 141.

11. *Ibid.,* p. 142.

12. Thomas, *op. cit.*

13. *Ibid.*

14. Ashley L. Schiff, *Fire and Water: Scientific Heresy in the Forest Service* (Cambridge: Harvard University Press, 1962).

15. G. M. Woodwell, "What Level of Life?" *Bulletin No. 76,* Yale University School of Forestry, 1970, pp. 18–29.

CHAPTER 2

1. During the period January to April of 1970, for example, *Look, Time, Newsweek, Life, Fortune* and many other popular and professional journals either devoted issues to or did feature stories on ecology. Since then, there has been a constant bombardment via the mass media.

2. The science of ecology emphasizes the "web of life," i.e., man is just one species in a complex and interrelated biosphere. Hence, most ecologists reject the anthropocentric focus of much of traditional theology. When the ecologically minded do theology, they construct a new kind of "nature mysticism." See Frederick Elder, *Crisis in Eden* (Nashville: Abingdon, 1970), and the works of ecological scientists, e.g.,

Loren Eiseley and Ian McHarg. Man's peculiar responsibility to transform as well as to protect the natural order is, unfortunately, de-emphasized. In addition, most of the writings on an ethic of ecology devote almost no space to the special environmental problems of the poor. See F. F. Darling and J. P. Milton (eds.), *Future Environment of North America* (New York: The Natural History Press, 1966).

3. See T. Roszak, *The Making of a Counter Culture* (New York: Doubleday, 1969), for a brilliant explication of the youth movement. His work stands in sharp contrast to black theologians and other black writers who emphasize political and economic justice in a racist society.

4. This comment was made at a meeting held by the Boston Industrial Mission in April, 1970, between Boston Area Ecology Action and the Massachusetts Welfare Rights Organization.

5. The words are an "almost exact" quotation from an address made by Eugene Jones in Trinity Lutheran Church, Roxbury Massachusetts, during a memorial service for the late Dr. Martin Luther King, Jr., on April 4, 1970. They were enthusiastically received by the predominantly black audience.

6. Delivered to the U.S. Congress on January 22, 1970, and reproduced in *Vital Speeches,* February 1, 1970, pp. 226–29.

7. Quoted in *Earth Day—The Beginning* (New York: Bantam, 1970), p. 216. The Boston Industrial Mission has explored with Dr. Wiley and others from the National Welfare Rights Organization and ecology groups possible avenues of cooperation between the two movements.

8. See Kenneth Boulding, "Economics of the Coming Spaceship Earth" in G. De Bell, *The Environmental Handbook* (New York: Ballantine, 1970), pp. 96–101. See also the brochure, "The Boston Industrial Mission at Mid-Decade," Boston Industrial Mission, Cambridge, Mass., May, 1970.

9. René Dubos, *So Human an Animal* (New York: Charles Scribner and Sons, 1968).

10. Figures are from the Bureau of Labor Statistics, Department of Labor, Washington, D.C.

11. Increased economic growth means a bigger pie, and a bigger slice for all. Most economists argue that economic growth avoids class tensions, since everyone appears to be getting more even if the relative gaps remain unchanged. For the relationships between economic growth and employment, see "Technology and the American Economy," *National Commission on Technology, Automation, and Economic Progress* (Washington, D.C.: U.S. Government Printing Office, 1966). See also economic textbooks, especially those written by Keynesian economists. For the futility of endless economic growth, see E. Mishan, *Technology and Growth: The Price We Pay* (New York: Praeger, 1970).

12. For an insightful analysis and critique of income distribution, see G. Kolko, *Wealth and Power in America* (New York: Praeger, 1962).

13. See Lincoln H. and Alice T. Day, *Too Many Americans* (Boston: Houghton Mifflin, 1964), p. 31.

14. See Charles Park, *Affluence in Jeopardy: Minerals and the Political Economy* (San Francisco: Freeman, Cooper and Co., 1968), and P. Jalée, *The Pillage of the Third World,* trans. Mary Klopper (New York: Monthly Review Press, 1968).

15. See Lynn White, "The Historical Roots of Our Ecologic Crisis," *Science* (March 10, 1967), for an indictment of the Christian tradition. Man is the egocentric manipulator who cuts himself off from nature. White calls for a new theological vision, one which sees St. Francis of Assisi as the patron saint of ecology.